T0173837

Perspectives
on Information

Routledge Studies in Library and Information Science

Perspectives
on Information

Edited by Magnus Ramage
and David Chapman

Routledge
Taylor & Francis Group
New York   London

First published 2011
by Routledge
711 Third Avenue, New York, NY 10017

Simultaneously published in the UK
by Routledge
2 Park Square, Milton Park, Abingdon, Oxon OX14 4RN

Routledge is an imprint of the Taylor & Francis Group, an informa business

Typeset in Sabon by IBT Global.

Library of Congress Cataloging-in-Publication Data

Perspectives on Information / edited by Magnus Ramage, David Chapman.
p. cm. — (Routledge Studies in Library and Information Science ; 9)
Includes bibliographical references and index.
1. Information theory.   I. Ramage, Magnus (Magnus Alastair), 1970–   II. Chapman, David (David Alan), 1958–
Q360.P387 2011
003'.54—dc22
2010050148

ISBN13: 978-0-415-88410-5 (hbk)
ISBN13: 978-0-203-81450-5 (ebk)

Contents

Figures and Tables

FIGURES

TABLES

Acknowledgements

The editors and a number of the authors of this book are members of the Society and Information Research Group (SIRG) at the Open University (OU). The stimulation of that research environment, the contribution from fellow members of SIRG and the support of the Communication and Systems Department of the OU are gratefully acknowledged.

1 Introduction

Magnus Ramage and David Chapman

THE CRUCIAL ROLE OF INFORMATION IN SOCIETY

> Information is everything, and everything is information.
>
> (Beckett, 1971, p.103)

We live in a world suffused with information. From our bank records to our lists of friends, from our music collections to the genetic sequence of our bodies—many things which were perceived as physical objects are now widely understood through their information content.

Consider music as a straightforward example. There was a time before recording when music couldn't be separated from people—whether singing or playing an instrument, it was a person or persons doing it. Musical scores provided instructions, but the music required people. Technology broke that tie, and music was available from an object, whether it was a musical box, pianola, a gramophone, tape or a compact disc (CD). The fact that the encoding on a CD was digital was a significant departure from analogue records and tapes, but it wasn't one that necessarily had an impact on the user. The music was tied to a physical object even if it was a digital CD instead of an analogue record. Today, however, music floats free. You can download a file and use it wherever you want, transferring between laptop and MP3 player, television (TV) and mobile phone. Or you don't even bother downloading the file, you just listen online whenever you want on your computer at the desk or via your smartphone.

Music on a phone draws attention to a consequence of digitisation that has been developing since the telephone network started to use digital technology in the 1980s and which is often referred to as *convergence*. Originally, it was about the convergence of telecommunications and computing (telephone exchanges became giant computers, and computer data was sent over telephone links), but now all sorts of things converge because they all use digital technology. Taking telephone calls is only a small part of what a mobile phone does now. As well as playing music, it takes photographs, gets you the train timetables and allows you to pay for your parking. There's little point in enumerating everything you can do because there will be lots more that can be done with it in only a matter of months, and anyway sooner or later it will probably some different gadget doing all these things—the concept of a 'mobile phone' may itself soon be out of date. The message, though, is that more and more of these things are information, and the physical technology that gets them to us is incidental, or at least is conceptually separate from the information.

Talk of what can be done with a mobile phone puts the emphasis on the individual, especially as a consumer. That is not the only area in which the focus on information is increasing though. Government documents are replaced by online information, passports are supplemented by biometric data, and movements are tracked by closed-circuit television (CCTV; for good or ill). Many have argued that the Internet will reshape democratic debate, and some evidence can be seen that this is already happening (as discussed by Castells, 2009). Frequently quoted examples include the bottom-up nature of the Obama presidential campaign in the United States in 2008 and the organising of the opposition in Iran via Twitter in 2009, although the popular story of transformation through technology in both of these cases has been questioned.

Examples such as these lead many to describe our current period as the information age and the information society. Although there is a need to be careful how we interpret these sentiments and the conclusions that we draw from them, at the very least, we need to explore what is behind them. In particular, it is important to decipher what people are talking about when they refer to 'information', since it is far from obvious. In the words of Fred Dretske, quoted by Holwell in Chapter 6 of this book:

> It is much easier to talk about information than it is to say what it is you are talking about . . . A surprising number of books, and this includes textbooks, have the word information in their title without bothering to include it in their index. It has come to be an all-purpose word, one with suggestive power to fulfil a variety of descriptive tasks. (1981, p. ix)

By exploring information from a variety of perspectives, this book aims to contribute to the understanding of information.

INFORMATION THROUGH MANY ACADEMIC LENSES

An awareness of the need to understand information has arisen in many academic disciplines.

Pre-eminently, perhaps, engineering and technology, specifically computer and communications technologies, have led the way, since these technological developments have, if not created the information age, at least been the main enabler. It may be that many working on developments in information and communication technologies (ICTs) have done so with little reflection on the significance of their output, but others certainly have been fully aware of it, with many of them as enthusiastic evangelists for the possibilities opened up by the new technologies (e.g. Shirky, 2008). The rise of the Internet and Web, and the significant changes upon society that have arisen through their development, have led to much hyperbole, especially about the dominant role of information, but it has also led to a richer and more considered debate about the history and the future of the Web (see, for example, Naughton, 2000; Berners-Lee et al., 2006). Yet as some technologists argue, the Web is not just changing the *role* of information but also the *nature* of information, or at least our relationship to it—as Weinberger vividly writes, "As we invent new principles of organisation that make sense in a world of knowledge freed from physical constraints, information doesn't just want to be free. It wants to be *miscellaneous*" (2007, p.7).

Within social sciences, the concept of the Information Society figures highly as a topic of investigation—understandably given that 'society' is the central area of study of sociology, and given the primacy of information. The term 'information society' is in widespread use in popular writing and in government circles (the European Commission has long had a Director General for the Information Society). It has been analysed by a generation of social scientists, starting with the work of the economist Fritz Machlup (1962) who first wrote of the "knowledge industries" and continuing through later writers such as Daniel Bell (1973), with his work on post-industrial society, and Manuel Castells (1996) with his work on theories of the network society. For some writers, the information society is equated with globalisation, for others, with postmodernism. The concept has been problematised by a number of writers in the social sciences—as Webster observes, "what strikes one in reading the literature on the information society is that so many writers operate with undeveloped definitions of their subject" (2002, p.8). Nonetheless, the concept is one that continues to be of some relevance and debate within the social sciences.

The nature and role of information in business and management has inevitably received a lot of attention. Because of the economic nature of the discourse around the information society, much of the work in that area has had a strong influence upon business and management, albeit in a more populist vein—it was Peter Drucker (1969), working within the field of management, who coined the term 'knowledge worker'. As with other fields, but especially so given the nature of the popular business literature, one strand of writing has been strongly utopian and determinist, exemplified by works such as *The Death of Distance* (Cairncross, 1997) and *We-Think* (Leadbeater, 2008).

The field of information systems, which sits between technology and management, takes information as its primary concept, and thus the nature of information is highly significant to the field. Most information systems textbooks have a section labelled 'what is information'.

Nonetheless, as Checkland and Holwell (1998) observe, information is poorly analysed within the field, partly due to an implicit assumption that information is something tangible, the equivalent of a physical object that can be stored and processed within an information system. In many ways, information systems is still coming to terms with understanding its fundamental concept.

The humanities too have been exploring the possibilities opened up by information technologies, and the consequences of new ways of working—the term 'digital humanities' is much in vogue within a range of disciplines. The typical research method of a historian or literary critic, painstakingly working through archives or texts, has been transformed by the ubiquity of digital texts. Even more obvious have been the changes to library science, and more generally the change in the understanding of books (as discussed later in this book, in Chapter 8 by Foster-Jones).

A book that has brought popular attention to the impact of the changing understanding of information, as opposed to the impact of information technologies, is Hans Christian von Baeyer's *Information: The New Language of Science* (2003). Although it is by no means universal in science, there is increasing awareness, especially in physics and biology, that the language of information provides a new tool for a scientific understanding of the world. Within biology there is both the growth of bioinformatics, with things like the human genome project from which we now have what might be thought of as a complete specification of a human being stored as a digital code and biosemiotics, which explores the meaning of signs in the biological world.

As people in all these different disciplines explore the nature and impact of information, others have been seeking a unified theory of information. This endeavour has been largely the work of philosophers, such as Luciano Floridi (2010) and Wolfgang Hofkirchner (2010). With information being discussed in so many different disciplines, seeking a unified theory is fraught with difficulties. There is no *a priori* reason to suppose that the word means the same thing when used in different contexts, so a single definition of the word might be impossible. Floridi's approach has been to come up with a categorisation which encompasses a range of different types of information (Floridi, 2010).

APPROACH OF THIS BOOK

Rather than seeking a unified theory of information, this book is taking its cue from von Baeyer's insight that information is a new *language* of science. We, however, argue that it is a language of much more than science, and this book has contributors from a range of disciplines. All have written about information, or about the new impacts of information, in their own fields of interest, and they have written in a deliberately accessible style aimed at presenting insights from their field to workers in other disciplines. In this way the book is to be considered a contribution to an interdisciplinary *conversation* about information. By exposing readers to the language of information as spoken in a range of disciplines, we aim to help them contribute both to the ongoing interdisciplinary exploration into the nature of information and to the enriching of their own disciplines through the insights that information offers.

We start in Chapter 2 with a historical perspective, specifically the birth of the current conception of information within the field of cybernetics. Magnus Ramage discusses the birth of cybernetics in the late 1940s and contrasts two competing models of information that arose around the same time within cybernetics and which he argues are still pervasive. These models are a 'hard' view, which treats information as an object in its own right and a 'soft' view, which regards the context and meaning of information as crucial.

Chris Bissell continues the historical perspective in Chapter 3 but in a somewhat different way. He argues that the popular concept of 'the information revolution' is highly misleading, in several respects. In particular, he looks at the long history of information and communication technologies and the ways in which they have previously both shaped, and been shaped by, the societies in which they arose. Bissell's writing is a particularly valuable counter to some of the utopian and deterministic writing about information that we referred to earlier.

Both Ramage and Bissell talk of the importance of the work of Claude Shannon, who is often described as 'the father of information theory'. In Chapter 4, David Chapman describes Shannon's work in more detail, and looks at the contentious question of whether Shannon's concept of information has any relevance to semantic information. Chapman draws on metaphors of layering, as used by engineers for layered models of communication systems, together with insights from semiotics, to suggest a way of thinking that links the two.

Semiotics is the main field that John Monk draws on in Chapter 5. He describes the functions of signs and how they are used by institutions. He suggests that 'information' is a word that comes into the vocabulary to talk about the sign games of institutions.

Both Sue Holwell in Chapter 6 and Paul Lefrere in Chapter 7 are interested in how information can inform purposeful action. Holwell comes from a background in Information Systems and explores what constitutes meaningful information in a social or organisational context. She introduces a hierarchy of concepts: data, capta, information and knowledge.

Lefrere describes the concept of 'exformation', the knowledge needed to make sense of a message but which is not sent because it is already known to both the sender and the recipient. He describes how messages sent between group members will be unintelligible to outsiders because they do not share the exformation.

Juanita Foster-Jones in Chapter 8 describes the changing nature of libraries, and the changing role of librarians, with the impact of Web 2.0. It can be seen as a 'case study' of the consequences of information being freed from a material object, as books cease to need a body of paper and card.

Chapter 9 by Paul Piwek explores information in the context of human dialogue. Drawing on the insights of linguists, logicians, computer scientists and philosophers, Piwek equates information flow with context change and finds that effective information flow is a cooperative endeavour, and one that is dependent on the existing context.

Chapter 10 is the only chapter in this book which looks specifically at information in physical science. In it, Tony Nixon writes about information in quantum physics. He presents a simple explanation—as simple as anything can be in quantum physics—of how quantum information differs from classical information, and he talks about the concept of the quantum bit, the qubit. He briefly explains how quantum cryptography works, discusses some aspects of quantum computers and touches on the problems of real-world interpretations of quantum theory.

The changing nature of information means that the ways of dealing with it have to change too. In Chapter 8, in which Foster-Jones looks at libraries, we see one example of the response to that change. In Chapter 11 by Ray Corrigan we see some of the problems that a failure to cope with changes can generate. Corrigan looks at the development of public policy on information, and, based around a case study of the United Kingdom's (UK's) Digital Economy Act, explores the lobbying and interest groups that are involved and the generally unsatisfactory outcomes.

The final chapter, the Conclusion in Chapter 12, extracts some common themes from the book and suggests some initial insights that emerge from the conversation in this collection.

BIBLIOGRAPHY

Beckett, J.A. (1971) *Management Dynamics: The New Synthesis*, New York, McGraw-Hill.

Bell, D. (1973) *The Coming of Post-Industrial Society: A Venture in Social Forecasting*, New York, Basic Books.

Berners-Lee, T., Hall, W., Hendler, J., Shadbolt, N. and Weitzner, D.J. (2006) 'Creating a Science of the Web', *Science*, vol. 313, no. 5788, pp.769–771.

Cairncross, F. (1997) *The Death of Distance*, London, Orion.

Castells, M. (1996) *The Rise of the Network Society*, Oxford, Blackwell.

Castells, M. (2009) *Communication Power*, Oxford, Oxford University Press.

Checkland, P.B. and Holwell, S.E. (1998) *Information, Systems and Information Systems: Making Sense of the Field*, Chichester, John Wiley and Sons.

Dretske, F.I. (1981) *Knowledge and the Flow of Information*, Oxford, Blackwell.

Drucker, P. (1969) *Age of Discontinuity: Guidelines to Our Changing Society*, New York, Harper and Row.

Floridi, L. (2010) *Information: A Very Short Introduction*, Oxford, Oxford University Press.

Hofkirchner, W. (2010) *Twenty Questions about a Unified Theory of Information*, Litchfield Park, Arizona, Emergent Publications.

Leadbeater, C. (2008) *We-Think*, London, Profile.

Machlup, F. (1962) *The Production and Distribution of Knowledge in the United States*, Princeton, New Jersey, Princeton University Press.

Naughton, J. (2000) *A Brief History of The Future: Origins of the Internet*, London, Orion Books.

Shirky, C. (2008) *Here Comes Everybody: The Power of Organizing without Organizations*, London, Allen Lane.

von Baeyer, H.C. (2003) *Information: The New Language of Science*, London, Weidenfeld and Nicolson.

Webster, F. (2002) *Theories of the Information Society*, 2nd ed., London, Routledge.

Weinberger, D. (2007) *Everything Is Miscellaneous: The Power of the New Digital Disorder*, New York, Times Books.

A website with further information and links associated with this book can be found at http://www.perspectiveson.info/.

2 Competing Models of Information in the History of Cybernetics

Magnus Ramage

INFORMATION AT THE MACY CONFERENCES

The information society has always been with us, as argued by Bissell in Chapter 3 of this book. Information, through its changing forms and media, has been always been a guiding principle for the organisation of society and for many different forms of scientific understanding. Nonetheless, a key development in the centrality of information to society occurred in the late 1940s and early 1950s with the birth of the field of cybernetics.

The development of cybernetics in its Anglo-American form took shape during a set of conferences organised by the Macy Foundation. The Macy Conferences on Cybernetics, as they ultimately became known, were a series of ten, two-day meetings between 1946 and 1953, largely held in New York City. As Bissell (2010) observes, there are other historical traditions within cybernetics, especially within Germany and Russia, but the Macy Conferences formed a dominant strain within cybernetics in the English-speaking world, and it is with that tradition that I will be concerned here.

The conferences had two aims: to explore feedback processes and circular causality within a range of disciplines and to explore common behaviours between biological, social and artificial systems. They were thus explicitly interdisciplinary. The list of participants in the conferences is extraordinary: among the better known were Norbert Wiener (mathematics), Gregory Bateson (anthropology), John von Neumann (physics and mathematics), Claude Shannon (communications), Warren McCulloch (neurophysiology), Margaret Mead (anthropology), Kurt Lewin (social psychology), Alex Bavelas (social psychology), Heinz von Foerster (physics), Ralph Gerard (neurophysiology) and Wolfgang Köhler (psychology).

The Macy conferences occurred at a key moment in the development of a number of fields for several different reasons. First, coming as they did immediately after the Second World War, interdisciplinarity was part of the experience of many researchers. Second, the development of the digital computer during and immediately after the war acted both as an inspiration and as resource for the development of a wide range of theories on the nature of mind, control, communications and behaviour. Third, they reflected a growing view of the importance of circular causality across many fields—as Margaret Mead later said, "there wasn't a person in the country who was thinking hard about problems who didn't have a folder somewhere marked something like 'circular systems'" (Brand, 1976). Fourth, they drew on a number of key wartime research projects which all focused on control and communication processes within both man-made systems and biological systems.

These ideas came together in different ways from each of the key contributors to the conferences, but they had their most public expression in the work of Norbert Wiener, who coined the term 'cybernetics' and wrote a celebrated (albeit dense and difficult) book on the subject (Wiener, 1948). Wiener's work on cybernetics began with two research projects: on feedback within human and animal physiology and on the building of control systems for anti-aircraft weaponry during World War 2. Wiener and his collaborators brought together these ideas in a crucial article in 1943 (Rosenbleuth et al., 1943), and he subsequently developed them in his 1948 book. The subtitle of this book was 'control and communication in the animal and the machine', and these two pairs of linked concepts were key to his understanding of the new field.

The Macy conferences created more than one new discipline—as well as cybernetics itself, the fields of artificial intelligence, computational linguistics, complexity theory and family therapy owe much to the discussions in the Macy conferences. The conferences were full of strong argument by people from very different backgrounds, who all saw the importance of the newborn field of cybernetics but wanted to shape it in quite different ways. Nonetheless, the conferences were hugely influential, especially so in their influence on the developing concept of information.

I have written elsewhere both about the lives and key work of a number of the key Macy participants (Ramage and Shipp, 2009), and in Ramage (2009) I specifically contrasted the work of Norbert Wiener and Gregory Bateson, relating them to Donna Haraway's concept of the cyborg. My purpose in this chapter is not to focus so much on individuals as on ideas: on two concepts of information, which arose during the Macy conferences, and can be seen as continuous traditions.

The first (which in shorthand I refer to as 'hard' information, and has been dominant in technical domains) derives especially from the work of Norbert Wiener and Claude Shannon. The second (which I refer to as 'soft' information, and is more influential in social science) derives from the work of Gregory Bateson, Ross Ashby and to a lesser extent Donald Mackay. I will examine the origins of these two approaches in the early work of cybernetics, and then trace through some of their later implications within cybernetics and the disciplines it helped to create. In earlier work (Ramage, 2009) I referred to these traditions as two schools of thought in cybernetics, hard and soft cybernetics—my focus here is more closely on approaches to information rather than schools of cybernetics, but this is a fine distinction given that in the earlier work I argued that their approach to information was a key distinguishing feature of these two schools.

My argument in this chapter is that information is a contested concept; we can identify at least two highly influential ways to understand it that go back more than sixty years, and both of these approaches can equally be considered legitimate.

WIENER, SHANNON AND THE 'HARD' VIEW OF INFORMATION

The first and most prominent view of information within the cybernetics domain has been one that treats information as an object in its own right, removed from its original physical and cultural context. For example, information may have begun as a set of words in a book, but the words (once digitised) can be analysed independently of the physical book. This is a familiar phenomenon, as discussed elsewhere in this book—the way by which very many parts of the world that once had a largely physical form can now be seen as forms of information (such as books, music, money and even social networks). These can thus be treated analytically, using mathematical tools and looking at the ways in which the information is stored, processed and transmitted.

This perspective is crucial to the way modern society is organised and has enabled the development of information and communication technologies of all kinds. Nonetheless, it depends on what is at first sight a peculiar double manoeuvre: information was (and is) simultaneously disembodied and reified—it "lost its body" (Hayles 1999, p.2) in the sense of being taken out of its original physical context (disembodiment)—but was then treated as an object in its own right (reification). As Hayles further puts it, information is treated as "an entity distinct from the substrates carrying it . . . a kind of bodiless fluid that could flow between different substrates without loss of meaning or form" (1999, p.ix).

The hard view of information derives from the related work of Norbert Wiener and Claude Shannon in the late 1940s, as well as earlier work by Ralph Hartley. Shannon's theories and approach are covered in some detail in Chapter 4 of this book, by Chapman, and so my focus in this chapter is on the work of Wiener (who was more explicitly identified with cybernetics, although Shannon was a participant in three of the Macy conferences) and the links between Wiener and Shannon, rather than on Shannon's work directly.

For both Wiener and Shannon, information (and especially its transmission, which was Shannon's focus given his work for Bell Labs, the research arm of the telecoms firm AT&T) was treated using the mathematics of statistical mechanics. The information content of a message was treated in terms of its probability—a message that was more probable was held to carry less information—"the more probable the message, the less information it gives. Clichés, for example, are less illuminating than great poems" (Wiener, 1954, p.21).

Closely linked to probability in Wiener's mathematical work was a link between information and entropy (the degree of disorder in a physical system, a key concept in thermodynamics)—he regarded information as the opposite of entropy and referred to it as 'negentropy'. As he wrote, "just as the amount of information in a system is a measure of its degree of organisation, so the entropy in a system is a measure of its degree of disorganisation; and the one is simply the negative of the other" (Wiener, 1948, p.11).

This link between information and organisation was crucial for the parallels Wiener developed between machines and biological systems. Organisation became important in theoretical biology in the 1930s (not least through the work of Ludwig von Bertalanffy, the founder of general systems theory with which cybernetics would gradually converge). As Wiener's biographers have observed, "it was that new, dynamic quality of organisation that Wiener brought to his conception of information . . . he joined the animate and inanimate worlds, and completed his bridge across the no man's land of science" (Conway and Siegelman, 2005, p.190).

There were close parallels between Wiener and Shannon's treatments of information—both treated information as if it were an independent object, analysing it in terms of probability. A mutual acknowledgment of their links can be found in each author's work. Shannon writes that "communication theory is heavily indebted to Wiener for much of its basic philosophy and theory" (Shannon, 1948) and Wiener that "this idea occurred about the same time to several writers, among them the statistician R.A. Fisher, Dr Shannon of the Bell Telephone Laboratories, and the author" (Wiener, 1948, p.10). Indeed, the two worked closely together in the early 1940s (although Shannon was twenty years younger than Wiener). Wiener's collaborator Julian Bigelow later recalled that "in the time I was associated with Wiener, Shannon would come and talk to Wiener every couple of weeks and spend a hour or two talking with him" (Conway and Siegelman, 2005, p.126).

However, it cannot be denied that it is to Shannon that phrases like 'the father of information theory' are attributed (ironically, given that he consistently referred to his work as 'communication theory' and denied the anthropocentric implications of the term information)—it is Shannon's version of mathematical information that has been influential. This is particularly because he wrote his work in the context of digital telecommunications, an area that was to develop hugely in the following decades; it is striking that his work is still so widely quoted, with a modern writer like Vedral (2010) writing of quantum information theory in a way that draws heavily on Shannon's work.

A distinction between Shannon and Wiener's concepts of information was that Shannon confined his area of application of the concept to telecommunications, while Wiener was interested in a more general application. He wrote that "The process of receiving and of using information is the process of our adjusting to the contingencies of the outer environment, and of our living effectively within that environment. . . . To live effectively is to live with adequate information. Thus, communication and control belong to the essence of man's inner life, even as they belong to his life in society" (Wiener, 1954, pp.17–18).

Notwithstanding the reification process to which I have referred above, Wiener was very clear that information was not a physical concept and was quite different from energy in particular: "information is information, not matter or energy; no materialism which does not admit this can survive at the present day" (Wiener, 1948, p.155). However, for both Wiener and Shannon, the *meaning* of the information was not relevant. Shannon famously wrote that the "semantic aspects of communication are irrelevant to the engineering problem" (Shannon, 1948, p.379), and Wiener likewise took meaning as outside of his area of relevance. As Hayles (1999) observes, this was an appropriate choice in the context of telecommunications, because of the need to ensure that information remains stable as it moves from one context to another.

In fact, a current thinker within second-order cybernetics, Søren Brier, has observed that within the specific context of telecommunication, Shannon's choice made good sense and that it was Wiener's extension of these ideas to a wider context that caused problems:

> Shannon's information theory is thus a quantitative theory used on a set of messages that are presumed to be meaningful. It is a technical theory about how to quantify and mathematically model information as a tool but always operating on human social communication. As such it presents no problems. The problem arises with the reification of information by connecting it to thermodynamics, as Wiener did, that raises foundational problems that reflect back on the prerequisites for science itself. (Brier, 2008, p.236)

It was the absence of meaning from information that was the dividing line with the other main school of information within cybernetics that I will now move on to consider.

BATESON, MACKAY AND THE 'SOFT' VIEW OF INFORMATION

From the beginnings of cybernetics in the Macy conferences, an alternative view of information to the Wiener/Shannon hard view has also been present. This view finds the *context* of information to be highly important, especially its meaning and the people who work with it. This view closely links information with two other concepts that were later to become central to certain forms of cybernetics: that of the *observer* and the *mental processes* of those who create, share or make sense of the information.

It might seem that this view of information is created in opposition to the hard view described earlier, not least because that view is very widely known and widely associated with the techno-centrism that many associate with the term cybernetics. While the soft view of information has at times sat in opposition to the hard view, it also has its origins in the Macy conferences and other early work in cybernetics. This school is more diverse in its history than the hard school—it is especially associated with the early work of Gregory Bateson (who was a key participant in the Macy conferences), Donald Mackay and Ross Ashby (both of whom attended one Macy conference). It is connected with, but not identical to, the school that I have called "soft cybernetics" (Ramage, 2009), which includes the second-order cybernetics work led by Heinz von Foerster; the differences between this work and second-order cybernetics are discussed in my earlier paper. It is worth noting that Bateson, Mackay and Ashby were British, while Shannon and Wiener were American, although there is not an obvious link to national culture in either group's work.

Bateson's view of information is quite well-known, although it largely developed after the Macy conferences. It was most clearly expressed in a lecture he gave as late as 1970, but his ideas were present from the mid-1950s onwards. Bateson started from the concept of 'difference', a non-mathematical statement of Shannon's concept of information—the difference between multiple potential states. Drawing on the example of a piece of chalk, which Kant said contained an infinite number of potential states, Bateson extended the argument to difference:

> I suggest that Kant's statement can be modified to say that there is an infinite number of *differences* around and within the piece of chalk. . . . Of this infinitude, we select a very limited number, which become information. In fact, what we mean by information—the elementary unit of information—is a difference which makes a difference. (Bateson, 1972, p.453)

This last phrase, the "difference which makes a difference", is crucial to Bateson's understanding of information and distinguishes it clearly from Shannon and Wiener's concepts. For Bateson, true information is not present until meaning has been attributed to the difference by some kind of observer—until a process of selection has occurred. The concepts of information and communication were as closely linked for Bateson as they were for Shannon but in a broader way. During the latter part of the Macy conferences, Bateson's main research was on the psychological basis of communication, and he wrote during the conferences of the importance of information going beyond the simple system, arguing that

> Negative entropy, value, and information, are in fact alike in so far as the system to which these notions refer is the man plus environment, and in so far as, both in seeking information and in seeking values, the man is trying to establish an otherwise improbable congruence between ideas and events. (Ruesch and Bateson, 1951, p.179)

A key part of the distinction between Bateson and Wiener's concepts of information reflected their different disciplinary origins—Bateson in anthropology and psychology and Wiener in mathematics and engineering. Concepts of meaning are crucial to the social sciences—the great German cybernetic sociologist Niklas Luhmann (1990, p.21) later called meaning the "basic concept" of sociology—but of less relevance to technical subjects. However, meaning was also of crucial importance to the next information theorist I want to consider, Donald Mackay, who was a physicist at Kings College, London. While equally strongly based in mathematics—and just as keen to measure the amount of information in a given exchange—Mackay argued for a broader definition of information than Shannon and Wiener. In a paper at the eighth Macy conference in 1951 (republished in a 1969 collection), he distinguished between two approaches to information:

a) that of the physicist, "who wants to make a representation of physical events which he must not prejudge" (Mackay, 1969, p.159). This results in what Mackay referred to as scientific information, with two linked components—the structural information content (the number of different independent variables to be described) and the metrical information content (the weight of evidence about those variables).

b) that of the communications engineer, "whose task is to make a representation at the end of a communication channel, of something he already knows to be one member of a set of standard representations which he possesses" (Mackay, 1969, p.159). This results in what Mackay referred to as selective information, in that its principal goal is to select between a set of pre-determined elements—the approach taken by Shannon in particular.

From a historical point of view, it is worth remarking that Mackay's model of scientific information was developed independently of Shannon's ideas, rather than in reaction to them. Mackay argued further that the two components of scientific information were quantifiable, and he presented scales for measuring each of these components—'logons' to measure structural information content, drawing on earlier work by the physicist Dennis Gabor, and 'metrons' to measure metrical information content, drawing on the earlier work of the statistician R.A. Fisher (also drawn on by both Wiener and Shannon).

Katherine Hayles, in discussing Mackay's appearance at the Macy conferences and his differences from Shannon, argues that meaning was an

explicit part of his approach: "Mackay's model recognized the mutual constitution of form and content, message and receiver ... subjectivity, far
from being a morass to be avoided, is precisely what enables information
and meaning to be connected" (Hayles, 1999, p.56). However, the concept
was somewhat implicit at that stage, as he wrote quite explicitly in his
Macy paper that "the term 'information' means something quite distinct
from 'meaning'" (Mackay, 1969, p.160).

Following a year spent working in Warren McCulloch's lab, Mackay
moved his focus towards studying the way that the human brain worked in
its storage and processing of information, which was to occupy him much
more than his initial theory of information. However, within this context
he worked to expand the idea of Shannon's selective information content to
incorporate meaning, in particular that to the recipient. While noting that
selective information did not incorporate meaning by itself, he noted that
we might identify the richness of meaning of a set of information with "the
complexity of the selective operation (or of the features of the state of readiness organised by it)" (Mackay, 1953, p.194), and he presented a means to
quantify that complexity.

Partly because this later model required an understanding of the internal
state of the recipient's brain, something that was neither physically nor theoretically possible in the early 1950s, it was regarded by the physicists and
engineers of the time as simply too difficult to quantify, and so Shannon's
model became the standard approach. Mackay's approach is an intriguing alternative to the context-free ideas of Shannon, however, and Hayles
notes that as late as 1968, the information theorist Nicolas Tzannes tried
to build Mackay's ideas into a quantifiable theory of information transmission, arguing that "whereas Shannon and Wiener define information in
terms of what it *is*, Mackay defines it in terms of what it *does*" (Hayles,
1999, p.56).

A further thinker on information who combined human and technical
perspectives was the psychiatrist Ross Ashby, author of the first textbook
on cybernetics, creator of the concept of self-organisation and inventor of
an early working model of an electronic brain. At the core of Ashby's work
was the concept of 'variety', which relates to the number of distinct elements
of a set and which he notes is a concept "inseparable from that of 'information'" (Ashby, 1956, p.140). Variety in Ashby's work gained its greatest
application in his Law of Requisite Variety, which states that the complexity of a regulatory system (the amount of information it can handle) needs
to be as great as the complexity of the system that it is regulating.

While Ashby was comfortable with describing information in Shannon's
terms—he observes that it can be measured in bits—he stressed the importance of context in measuring variety. He wrote that "a set's variety is not
an intrinsic property of the set: the observer and his powers of discrimina-
tion may have to be specified if the variety is to be well defined" (Ashby,
1956, p.125)—a helpful involvement of the importance of the observer (a

key defining feature of second-order cybernetics, to which Ashby served as a key inspiration) in a quasi-mathematical manner. Indeed, he explicitly linked his conception of variety to Mackay's ideas on selective information content, writing that "throughout, we shall be exemplifying the thesis of D.M. MacKay: that quantity of information, as measured here, always corresponds to some quantity, i.e. intensity, of selection, either actual or imaginable" (Ashby, 1956, p.252).

It might seem that the distinction between hard and soft information (or between hard and soft cybernetics) is a fine one, linked more to discipline than to a specific conception. However, it is my contention that we can clearly see two models of information, present in cybernetics from their start, and differentiated around their understanding of the importance of meaning, context and to some extent the role of the observer. These forms of information, and of cybernetics, were to develop significantly in the decades following the Macy conferences, as I shall briefly outline in the next section.

THE LATER ROLE OF INFORMATION IN CYBERNETICS

The purpose of this chapter is to explore the early treatment of information within cybernetics, and thus it is not the place for a comprehensive treatment of later work within cybernetics. There are many discussions of various aspects of the history of cybernetics, such as Heims (1991), Dupuy (2000), Scott (2004), Ramage and Shipp (2009) and Harkin (2009). However, a brief overview of developments relating to the ideas discussed here will be useful.

There are many fields which have developed via Wiener's harder view of information and thus of cybernetics. I have already mentioned artificial intelligence and computational linguistics, and clearly fields such as robotics and prosthetics take direct inspiration from hard cybernetics. It is hard cybernetics that forms the template for the many uses of portmanteau terms involving the prefix 'cyber-' in popular culture (especially science fiction), from William Gibson's conception of cyberspace and cyberpunk, through the Cybermen of the television series *Dr Who*, to cyborgs such as in the film *The Terminator*.

However, James Harkin (2009) argues that hard cybernetics has had a strong influence on our society as well and that the way it handled and gave primacy to the concept of information, operating within feedback loops, has created a cultural and intellectual basis for the primacy of information discussed elsewhere in this book. In particular, Harkin argues that this has led to the pervasive use of information through Web technologies such as social networking. Tracing a link through the work of the media theorist Marshall McLuhan (strongly influenced by cybernetics), he observes that "the world we now inhabit is one in which messages are rapidly becoming the medium:

electronic messages sent back and forth between us at breakneck speed on a never-ending electronic information loop" (Harkin, 2009, p.xiii).

Harkin is very clear that this information loop derives directly from Wiener's conception of information and the importance he placed on feedback. He traces the way this process developed both through the military and through semi-utopian technologists such as Stewart Brand who created the *Whole Earth Catalog* which eventually led to publications such as *Wired* magazine as well as the early but influential virtual community, the WELL. He argues that "as our enthusiasm for life on an electronic information loop has spread outwards into the culture it has influenced our perspective and given us some thrilling new ways of looking at the world" (Harkin 2009, p.249). Like Wiener himself, Harkin regards this information loop as having both positive and negative aspects, arguing that

> Cybernetics has brought us a long way, but now that its global information loop is fully built it is in danger of leaving us lost. Its gurus were so mesmerised by the medium that they made the mistake of trying to push us into it head first, of trying to remake us in its image rather than the other way around. Now we need to spend some time thinking about the message. . . . If we use the medium for our own purposes rather than following slavishly in its thrall, we can imagine new ways of working, exciting new kinds of art and culture, new ways of organising ourselves and getting things done. (Harkin, 2009, p.256)

The soft view of information has likewise led to many different applications, in particular in the fields of family therapy, human communication and management theory. Gregory Bateson took and developed his ideas of information through studying communication patterns in both psychiatric patients and animals. This work led to an understanding of mental processes as existing on multiple levels (the concept of meta-communication), governed by paradoxes and taking place within a wider systems than just that of the individual. He led a research programme in Palo Alto, California, which formulated the 'double bind' theory of schizophrenia. This theory (at the time highly influential) looks at multiple levels of communication and argues that schizophrenia can arise when information at some levels is strongly in conflict with that at different levels but all are required to be held true simultaneously.

Bateson's work on communication was taken up and developed by his collaborators in Palo Alto, many of whom were the founders of the Mental Research Institute where significant early work on family systems therapy developed. Their work on human communication and family therapy (e.g. Watzlawick et al., 1967) drew quite explicitly on Bateson's conception of communication at multiple levels. Others within family and individual therapy have drawn heavily on Bateson's model of information, notably Mara Selvini-Palazolli and her colleagues in the Milan School of family therapy

(Stagoll, 2005); and in a different way the radical psychiatrist R.D. Laing, much of whose work is strongly based on Bateson's conception of paradox and levels (e.g. Laing, 1970). In later life, Bateson became very concerned that faulty mental models and epistemologies were contributing directly to environmental degradation, an idea deeply linked to his view of information and which has fed into the environmental movement (as recounted by his daughter Mary Catherine Bateson, 1972).

The work of Ross Ashby had a considerable effect on the field of cybernetics. His approach to information was taken up heavily within the field of management and organisation theory in two separate ways. First, his concept of variety (which as discussed above is closely related to information) was crucial to the work of Stafford Beer, creator of the field of 'management cybernetics' (e.g. Beer, 1979). Second, his concept (not previously discussed in this article) of ultrastability—self-regulation of a system's behaviour in response to its environment—formed the basis of Argyris and Schön's (1978) distinction between single- and double-loop learning and hence their theory of organisational learning.

Mackay's work on information has been less taken up by later theorists and practitioners, partly because of the difficulty of implementing his ideas, but he left a rich seam of ideas, and many pieces of work on "information, mechanism and meaning" (Mackay, 1969). Gradually this work is being drawn upon—a recent article by Kettinger and Li (2010) builds on his concept of information as "the state of conditional readiness" (Mackay, 1969, p.22) to distinguish between the three classic terms of data, information and knowledge.

CONCLUSION

My aim in this chapter has been not so much to argue for the primacy of one approach over the other but to establish that both have roots deep in the history of cybernetics. It is often supposed, and even asserted, that there was a single original form of cybernetics (that of Wiener), from which various divergent forms have arisen, in reaction to the original. Likewise, it is frequently asserted in literature on information that Shannon's definition is the original form and that other ways of understanding information are reactive and secondary. I hope I have shown in this chapter that an alternative reading of the history of information within cybernetics is at least possible—that the soft view of information has been present within cybernetics from its earliest days, just as much as with the hard view of information.

It is possible to argue that my case above is too dualistic, that in practice the two versions of information are much closer together and the differences small. I have some sympathy with this view. The question as to the role of meaning in Shannon's theory is still an open one (and argued in somewhat different terms by Chapman in Chapter 4 of this book). Likewise, some of

Mackay's work could be placed within the hard view of information just as much as the soft. I have addressed the question of dualism in distinguishing between the works of Wiener and Bateson in Ramage (2009), and specifically tried to see a way out of this dualism via the feminist cyborg epistemology of Donna Haraway (1991). However, it seems clear to me that the question of meaning is absolutely crucial to an understanding of the development of the concept of information within cybernetics, and it is on that question that a clear distinction can be made between two competing models of information within cybernetics.

BIBLIOGRAPHY

Argyris, C. and Schön, D.A. (1978) *Organizational Learning: A Theory of Action Perspective*, Reading, Massachusetts, Addison-Wesley.

Ashby, W.R. (1956) *An Introduction to Cybernetics*, London, Chapman and Hall.

Bateson, G. (1972) *Steps to an Ecology of Mind*, Toronto, Chandler.

Bateson, M.C. (1972) *Our Own Metaphor: A Personal Account of a Conference on the Effects of Conscious Purpose on Human Adaptation*, New York, Knopf.

Beer, S. (1979) *The Heart of Enterprise*, Chichester, John Wiley.

Bissell, C. (2010) 'Not just Norbert', *Kybernetes*, vol. 39, no. 4, pp.496–509.

Brand, S. (1976) 'For God's Sake, Margaret: Conversation with Gregory Bateson and Margaret Mead', *CoEvolution Quarterly*, vol. 10, pp.32–44.

Brier, S. (2008) 'Bateson and Pierce on the Pattern that Connects and the Sacred', in Hoffmeyer, J. (ed.), *A Legacy for Living Systems: Gregory Bateson as Precursor to Biosemiotics*, Berlin, Springer, pp.229–256.

Conway, F. and Siegelman, J. (2005) *Dark Hero of the Information Age: In Search of Norbert Wiener, the Father of Cybernetics*, New York, Basic Books.

Dupuy, J.-P. (2000) *The Mechanization of the Mind: On the Origins of Cognitive Science*, Princeton, Princeton University Press.

Haraway, D. (1991) 'A Cyborg Manifesto: Science, Technology, and Socialist-Feminism in the Late Twentieth Century', in *Simians, Cyborgs and Women: The Reinvention of Nature*, New York, Routledge, pp.149–181.

Harkin, J. (2009) *Cyburbia: The Dangerous Idea That's Changing How We Live and Who We Are*, London, Little, Brown.

Hayles, N.K. (1999) *How We Became Posthuman: Virtual Bodies in Cybernetics, Literature, and Informatics*, Chicago, University of Chicago Press.

Heims, S.J. (1991) *Constructing a Social Science for Postwar America: The Cybernetics Group, 1946–1953*, Cambridge, Massachusetts, MIT Press.

Kettinger, W.J. and Li, Y. (2010) 'The Infological Equation Extended: Towards Conceptual Clarity in the Relationship between Data, Information and Knowledge', *European Journal of Information Systems*, vol. 19, no. 4, pp.409–421.

Laing, R.D. (1970) *Knots*, London, Tavistock Publications.

Luhmann, N. (1990) *Essays on Self-Reference*, New York, Columbia University Press.

Mackay, D.M. (1953) 'Operational Aspects of Some Fundamental Concepts of Human Communication', *Synthese*, vol. 9, no. 3/5, pp. 182–198.

Mackay, D.M. (1969) *Information, Mechanism, and Meaning*, Cambridge, Massachusetts, MIT Press.

Ramage, M. (2009) 'Norbert and Gregory: Two Strands of Cybernetics', *Information, Communication and Society*, vol. 12, no. 5, pp.735–749.

Ramage, M. and Shipp, K. (2009) *Systems Thinkers*, London, Springer.

Rosenbleuth, A., Wiener, N. and Bigelow, J. (1943) 'Behavior, Purpose and Teleology', *Philosophy of Science*, vol. 10, no. 1, pp.18–24.

Ruesch, J. and Bateson, G. (1951) *Communication: The Social Matrix of Psychiatry*. New York, W.W. Norton.

Scott, B. (2004) 'Second-Order Cybernetics: An Historical Introduction', *Kybernetes*, vol. 33, no. 9/10, pp.1365–1378.

Shannon, C. (1948) 'A Mathematical Theory of Communication', *Bell System Technical Journal*, vol. 27, no. 3, pp.379–423, 623–656.

Stagoll, B. (2005) 'Gregory Bateson (1904–1980): A Reappraisal', *Australian and New Zealand Journal of Psychiatry*, vol. 39, no. 11/12, pp.1036–1045.

Vedral, V. (2010) *Decoding Reality: The Universe as Quantum Information*. Oxford, Oxford University Press.

Watzlawick, P., Beavin, J.H. and Jackson, D.D. (1967) *Pragmatics of Human Communication: A Study of Interactional Patterns, Pathologies, and Paradoxes*, New York, W.W. Norton and Company.

Wiener, N. (1948) *Cybernetics: Or Control and Communication in the Animal and the Machine*, Cambridge, Massachusetts, MIT Press.

Wiener, N. (1954) *The Human Use of Human Beings: Cybernetics and Society* (revised ed.), Garden City, New York, Doubleday.

3   'The Information Revolution'
Taking a Long View

Chris Bissell

INTRODUCTION

The historian and sociologist of science Steven Shapin opened his widely acclaimed book *The Scientific Revolution* with the words: "There was no such thing as the Scientific Revolution, and this is a book about it". He went on to write:

> Some time ago [. . .] historians announced the real existence of a coherent, cataclysmic, and climactic event that fundamentally and irrevocably changed what people knew about the natural world and how they secured knowledge of it. It was the moment at which the world was made modern, it was a Good Thing, and it happened sometime during the period from the late sixteenth to the early eighteenth century. It was, of course, the Scientific Revolution. (Shapin, 1996, p.1)

Shapin's tongue-in-cheek opening words prompt a number of questions about the current 'information revolution':

- is it a real, coherent, cataclysmic and climactic event?
- has it fundamentally and irrevocably changed our view of the world?
- has it made the world *post*-modern?
- when did it happen?

In his book, Shapin noted that scholars had questioned each word in the phrase 'the scientific revolution'. He is not the only historian or sociologist of science and technology to use this approach as the starting point for an essay. Bruno Latour famously remarked in a keynote address at a conference on actor-network theory: "There are four things that do not work with actor-network theory; the word actor, the word network, the word theory and the hyphen!" (Latour, 1999, p.15).

In this chapter I shall attempt to take a similar approach to Shapin's for the phrase 'the information revolution'. I shall look at the words in order of difficulty, starting with the easiest, *revolution*, and ending with possibly the most problematic, *the* (in the sense that it implies a single and unique event that is very difficult to pin down).

REVOLUTION

The word 'revolution' has an interesting history. Its original meaning of a turning, or a periodically repeating cycle, seems to have been applied only comparatively late to political events and at first in the sense of "fortune's wheel" (Shapin, 1996, p.3). That is, a political or social revolution was not necessarily a radical overturning or reordering of things, but rather a potentially repeating change rather like an economic cycle. The modern meaning of the word as we use it when we speak of an industrial, scientific, political—or, of course, an '*information* revolution'—dates back to the *philosophes* of the French Enlightenment. It may well have been applied to the notion of a revolution in science before being used to describe irreversible political events.

A name that must be mentioned when considering revolutions in science or technology is that of Thomas Kuhn, whose 1962 book *The Structure of Scientific Revolutions* (Kuhn, 1962) was extraordinarily influential in the philosophy and sociology of science and technology, and who was unwittingly responsible for the tendency of so many people to use the term 'paradigm shift' in a rather too casual way. Kuhn attempted to distinguish carefully between 'normal science' and 'revolutionary science'. Only when the pursuit of normal science within a prevailing paradigm—that is, a particular conceptual worldview—led to insurmountable inconsistencies, paradoxes or absurdities did an intellectual crisis occur which resulted in the replacement of one paradigm with another. We should be rather cautious, then, in applying the terms 'revolution' or 'paradigm shift' even to what appear at first sight to be enormous scientific or technological changes.

One of the most striking features of the rhetoric about 'the information revolution' is the way we are promised a utopia. Information and communication technologies, we are told, lead to virtually unlimited access to information and entertainment, instantaneous communication with anyone in the world, increased leisure and quality of life and even new, improved, forms of society. But there is nothing new about technological utopias.

A book was published in 1852 entitled *The Silent Revolution. Or, the Future Effects of Steam and Electricity upon the Condition of Mankind*, by Michael Angelo Garvey. It is a fantastic utopian romp through transport, commerce, superstition, education and the need for a universal language. Communication and Information rule. Here is the author's synopsis of the first chapter:

> Achievements of science: the power it bestows on mankind.—Illustrations of the energy and adaptation of steam in subserving human

purposes: its applications and benefits.—Locomotion by steam: its effects in developing enterprise.—Electricity: its probable destination as a channel of intelligence: general ideas of its power as an agent of communication.—The electric telegraph: its wonderful properties; annihilates time; unaffected by position. (Garvey, 1852, p.iii)

Steam and electricity, then, would bring about a utopia built on perfect communication. Indeed, "the union of mankind will be signalized by one form of speech, as it was at first before their dispersion" (ibid., p.xii) and "The free concourse of individual minds is the origin and mainspring of all social improvements . . . facilities for intercourse must always hold the first rank, and next to them the power of transmitting thought and intelligence with certainty" (ibid., p.15).

Incidentally, it is worth remarking on Garvey's choice of the phrase "annihilates time". The 'annihilation of time and space', or a variant of it, is a phrase that we hear repeated time after time in connection with claims for 'the information revolution', and has an interesting history. Perhaps the earliest mention of it in connection with a communications system is in the argument following Rowland Hill's proposal for the Penny Post in the 1830s. To some, the notion of a uniform rate was incomprehensible:

> The intrinsic value of the conveyance of a letter is exactly equal to the time, trouble and expense which is saved to the correspondent [. . .] The gods must annihilate both time and space before a uniform rate of postage can be reasonable or just.
> J.W. Crocker, *Quarterly Review*, 1839, quoted in Gregory (1987, p.133).

Yet the following year, the gods did just this: the Penny Post was introduced, and the postal system expanded beyond all expectations.

The utopian view of steam and the telegraph was widespread in the late nineteenth century. Charles Fraser, addressing the Mercantile Library Association of Charleston, South Carolina said:

> An agent was at hand to bring everything into harmonious cooperation . . . triumphing over space and time . . . to subdue prejudice and to unite every part of our land in rapid and friendly communication; and that great motive agent was steam. (Quoted in Carey and Quirk, 1970, p.225)

And President McKinley, at the Pan-American Exposition, Buffalo, September 1901, described the benefits of steam and the electric telegraph in these words:

> God and man have linked the nations together. No nation can longer be indifferent to any other. And as we are brought more and more in

touch with each other, the less occasion is there for misunderstandings and the stronger the disposition, when we have differences to adjust in the court of arbitration, which is the noblest forum for the settling of international disputes. (Quoted in Carey and Quirk, 1970, p.406)

The rhetoric of steam and electricity in the second half of the nineteenth century thus bears a remarkable resemblance to the current rhetoric about 'the information revolution'. For an extensive discussion of the "industri-alisation of time and space" in the nineteenth century by the railways, see Schivelbusch (1986).

In the mid-twentieth century came the so-called 'electronics revolu-tion'—or even what Zbigniew Brzezinski (1970) called "technetronics", in a book that now appears to us a very peculiar product of its time. The benefits of 1960s technology included, according to him:

- greater devolution of authority
- massive diffusion of scientific and technical knowledge as a principal focus of American involvement in world affairs
- the elimination of the "twin insulants of time and space"
- reduction of social conflicts [. . .] and a move to a pragmatic prob-lem-solving approach to social issues

It seems, therefore, if there has been, or is, a technological revolution in the information and communication technologies, it is not obvious when or what it was or is. We are so used to wondering at the 'revolutionary' growth in per-sonal computer (PC) ownership, or Internet access, that we perhaps forget the rather similar growth of earlier network technologies (Odlyzko, 2000). Vari-ous writers have seen parallels between the early days of telegraphy and the recent growth of the Internet. Best known is Tom Standage's *The Victorian Internet: The Remarkable Story of the Telegraph and the Nineteenth Centu-ry's On-Line Pioneers* (Standage, 1998). In some ways telegraph technology was an even greater achievement, for the early telegraph companies had to install the complete network infrastructure, whereas the Internet could build on the existing telephone and data networks. In the early 1850s, telegraph traffic grew at an enormous rate, sometimes doubling annually. And even over a period of decades, a range of early communication technologies kept up approximately exponential growth.

Now, clearly, a note of caution is in order. The time scales of the growth of the postal service or telegraphy are a lot longer than the recent growth of the Internet or the mobile phone—although it is easy to forget that the Internet has been around for over forty years and the mobile phone for thirty. Furthermore the sheer numbers (of hosts, websites, e-mail messages, etc) associated with the expanding Internet are orders of magnitudes greater than those in the above examples. But it is also easy to forget that until recently, e-mail was not the quick, ubiquitous facility we are now accustomed to. In 1990, for example, I regularly experienced a delay of five hours or more for an e-mail message from the United Kingdom (UK) to be delivered to the Netherlands: it was impossible to have an exchange of communication during the working day. In contrast, the frequency and speed of postal deliveries in the late nineteenth century (admittedly within a single city) were highly impressive: there were often many postal and telegraph deliveries each day, allowing multiple exchanges between correspondents. What is certainly true is that the evolution of many communication technologies followed a broadly similar pattern: rapid, even explosive, initial growth—and just as radical reduction in costs to users. For example, in 1866 a telegram from New York to London using the first transatlantic cable cost $10 per word (over a week's manual wage); by 1868 it was down to $1.58 and by 1880 to 50¢ (Odlyzko, 2000).

If we should be cautious about applying the word 'revolution' to new technologies, we should also treat claims of the radical nature of such new technologies with some scepticism. David Edgerton, in his book *The Shock of the Old* remarks:

> More recently, analysts have tended to highlight what they see as a radical transition from an industrial society to a post-industrial, or information, society brought about through the actions of the digital computer and the internet. In this context, some economists have developed the idea that economic history has been shaped by a few 'general-purpose technologies'. The central ones are successively steam power, electricity and now ICT. How seriously should we take these claims for these technologies, and for their significance in these particular periods? The answer is that such accounts, for all that they reflect what we think we know, are not as well founded as might be supposed. (Edgerton, 2006, p.3)

INFORMATION

If the word 'revolution' is problematic, then the term 'information' is even more so. Indeed, this entire book is devoted to an examination of how the notion of information is perceived and employed in various disciplines.

In his book *The Cult of Information* Theodore Roszak wrote "Information has had a remarkable rags-to-riches career in the public vocabulary over the past forty years" (Roszak, 1986, p.x). Indeed, in the 1933 edition of the *Oxford English Dictionary*, the word referred primarily to personal data, to a piece of news or intelligence or to various specialised legal uses. But by the time the 1986 edition appeared, a remarkable transformation had taken place. In addition to traditional meanings, a plethora of new terms appears:

> *information* content, desk, explosion, flow, gap, office, service, storage, system, transfer, work, carrying, gathering, giving, seeking, bureau, officer, processing, retrieval, science, technology

and, of course, *'the information revolution'*. Roszak argues that this particular 'information explosion' is evidence of a 'widespread public cult', a 'fetish' of the notion of information.

The value judgments implicit in the word 'information' and related concepts will be considered briefly below. But first it is worth spending a little time examining what we mean by 'information', beginning with the distinction between data, information and knowledge. Many definitions have been given of the distinction—here is one:

> Information is comprised of data in context. Information viewed relative to other information and filtered by user and corporate experience and strategy is knowledge. (Cordes, 2000)

In practice, such distinctions are very often not made: the terms *data* processing and *information* processing are often used interchangeably and *information* management and *knowledge* management often appear to be more or less synonymous. Let us explore these terms a little more.

It was in the immediate post-war period that the notion of 'information' began to take on its modern range of meanings. Particularly important was the work of Claude E Shannon, the 'father of information theory', who published his seminal paper *A Mathematical Theory of Communication* in 1948 (Shannon, 1948) and who died in February 2000. Shannon provided a generalised treatment of the transmission of symbols between a sender and a recipient through a noisy transmission channel which tended to corrupt the message. He introduced the notion of the quantifiable information content of a signal and showed that for a channel subject to a particular level of random noise there is a theoretical maximum rate at which a given message can be transmitted without error. (Shannon's work is discussed in detail by Chapman in Chapter 4 of this book and also by Ramage in Chapter 2.)

Shannon's paper led to the extremely fruitful discipline of information theory and is still of fundamental significance for the design of telecommunication systems. But in a way, his use of the term 'information' was unfortunate. In the Shannon sense, the information content of a message is a mathematical function of how likely that particular message is, and it is closely related to the concept of *entropy* in physics, which is a measure of the degree of randomness or disorder in a system. This is, intuitively, not unreasonable: a letter stating you have just won the lottery jackpot, for example, contains in a very real sense much more information than one asking you to pay your income tax. However, the probabilistic view is a far cry from everyday notions of information, and from an information-theoretical point of view, the 'meaning' of a message is irrelevant: Shannon's theory simply models the transmission of a sequence of symbols from sender to receiver. The 'information content' depends only on the probabilities of the individual symbols forming the message, and not what the symbols mean. Yet perhaps because of his use of the term 'information' and because of the hype surrounding ideas about cybernetics and automation in the immediate post-war period, models of the Shannon type were soon applied to biological, sociological and psychological contexts—sometimes with extremely useful results, but also sometimes excluding important aspects of the communication process which did not feature in the Shannon model.

It is instructive to consider briefly the Russian translation of Shannon's 1948 paper, since it was a translation not only into a different language but also into a completely different socio-political setting. In the Soviet Union *A Mathematical Theory of Communication* became *A Statistical Theory of Electrical Signal Transmission*. The Russian editor rid the paper of the words *information, communication* and *mathematical* entirely and put the word *entropy* in quotation marks. The words *information* and *communication*, with their anthropomorphic connotations, were completely unacceptable at that time within the Soviet Union, and using 'statistical' in place of 'mathematical' (arguably a more accurate description anyway) neatly avoided any accusation of an 'idealist' use of mathematics (Gerovitch, 2002). At the same time Shannon's use of the concept of *entropy* was distanced from the controversial discussions in Russia of this concept in physics and biology. For example, Lysenko, the later disgraced Soviet non-Darwinist biologist had condemned Erwin Schrodinger's book *What Is Life?* in which the concept of entropy was essential for explaining life processes. It would be a mistake to dismiss this anecdote as merely an example of totalitarian ideological extremism; rather, it should sensitise us to look a little more closely at our own linguistic behaviour in this field.

If the Shannon approach is really about the reliable transmission of data, when does data become information? Albert Borgmann (1999) came up with the following formulation in his book *Holding on to Reality. The Nature of Information at the Turn of the Millennium*:

> INTELLIGENCE provided, a PERSON is informed by a SIGN about some THING in a certain CONTEXT. (p.22)

"There is a pleasing symmetry to this relation", writes Borgmann, "at its centre is the sign, the fulcrum of the economy of information, and on it revolves the relation that mirrors the symmetry of humanity and reality, of intelligence and context, that undergirds every kind of epistemology [. . .]" (Borgmann, 1999, p.22). Borgmann is making some important points here, the first of which is the inherently cultural and contextual nature of information. He goes on to distinguish between different types of information:

- *information about reality* (reports, records, topographical signs, etc), which he terms *natural*
- *information for reality* (recipes, musical scores, circuit diagrams, etc) which he calls *cultural*
- *technological* information, or *information as reality* itself (a CD or a computer program, for example).

Borgmann's third category of information—what might be termed 'information as a commodity'—is certainly something that is making itself felt throughout cyberspace in particular. Indeed, the notion of 'information as a commodity' is perhaps at the heart of the current fashion for 'knowledge' management, the 'knowledge' society, the 'knowledge' economy and so on. The cultural baggage of words is important, and the words 'knowledge' or 'digital'—like 'modernisation' or 'fight against terror'—can cloak a wealth of value judgments. 'Knowledge' has so much more status than 'information'—and 'data' certainly carries no cachet.

THE

I will turn now to what I called possibly the most problematic aspect of the term 'the information revolution'. The use of the word 'the' implies that a completely unprecedented and unique event has occurred. The philosopher of technology Luciano Floridi, unusually in analyses of information technology, stresses the long history of 'the information revolution', dating back to the invention of writing in the Bronze Age in Mesopotamia (Floridi, 2010). Like most other writers, however, he emphasises developments since the 1950s as being categorically different and special. So let us move on to the word 'the', teasing out one or two of the multiple meanings of 'the information revolution'. There are a number of promising candidates:

- A 'communication revolution', perhaps, but I hope I have already indicated the difficulties of identification or location in time. Which is the greater revolution, our current ability to browse the Web, shop on line, subscribe to Facebook and Twitter—or the ability to send a telegraph from London to New Delhi in the mid 19th century rather than weeks of overland or sea travel?
- An 'electronics revolution'? But again, how do we analyse the relative significance of the thermionic valve (1920s), the transistor (late 1940s), the integrated circuit (1959) or the microprocessor (1971)?
- Or what about a 'battery revolution'? Without the amazing progress in battery technology, we would have no laptops, mobile phones or a whole range of portable electrical and electronic devices. But the notion of a 'battery revolution' seems rather comical, unlike an 'information revolution'. Perhaps it is because 'information' can

mean anything and everything, whereas a battery is just a bit too concrete and prosaic.

- Finally, is it an 'intergenerational revolution'? It is commonplace now to talk of the 'net generation' or 'digital natives', meaning young people who have always known the Web, and who are assumed to be much more at home with information and communication technology (ICT) than their elders; the latter are supposed to be struggling to a greater or lesser degree. Recent research, however, reveals a much more complex picture, with the so-called digital natives exhibiting a wide variety of competence in, and experience of, digital technologies, and not always the easy familiarity that is sometimes assumed (Jones et al., 2010).

Brian Winston (1998), in his book on the history of new technologies from the telegraph to the Internet, deals with the development of these and other technologies in great detail. He makes the bold claim of having identified a common model for the invention, development and dissemination of such technologies (including radio, television and video). Whether or not we agree with his model, one central element of his thesis is convincing: that the time-scale of all these developments was much longer than we often recognise, and, in retrospect, not always so revolutionary. So in this light let us now turn to the role of computers in 'the information revolution'.

Computational Revolution?

One of the claims for 'the information revolution' must be for a computational revolution, whether the electronic calculation of tax returns or the guidance systems for high-tech missiles. But if there has been a computational revolution, when did it take place, and what was it, exactly?

There is a long history of computing and calculating devices. One device that was well-known to every science school and university student until a few decades ago is the slide rule. An interesting feature of the slide rule is that it is an analogue, not a digital device. The numbers used in a calculation are represented by lengths along the rule, rather than as numbers in a mechanical calculator or digital computer. It is worth briefly considering some other analogue computing devices that played an important part in technological development this century—often considered revolutionary at the time, but largely forgotten today. First, however, let us be clear about analogue and digital techniques. As I have already suggested, the word 'digital' is part of the rhetoric of 'the information revolution'—it stands for everything modern and high-tech. A 'digital tyre inflator' was recently advertised—the only digital part, of course, was the tyre pressure display. And not a few people bought what they thought was a new, high-tech digital radio—only to find that the 'digital' applied only to the display and aspects of the electronics, not to the new broadcasting technology.

The French language uses the word *numérique* (numerical) where English uses 'digital' in the context of the information and communication technologies—for here 'digital' simply means expressing something as a number. A digital thermometer displays something like 20 degrees, for example, rather than the length of a column of mercury. Once expressed as a number, any quantity can be converted to a binary representation of 0s and 1s, and transmitted it in a variety of ways: a positive voltage for 1 and a negative voltage for 0 or a short flash of laser light for 1 and the absence of light for 0, which is the basis of optical fibre communication. One of the major advantages of digital techniques is their relative immunity to general degradation of the signal. Since it is necessary only to decide whether a received signal is a binary 0 or 1, provided the signal has not been degraded too much, it is easy to regenerate a completely 'clean' copy of the original binary sequence. (Hence all the current problems with digital piracy of music and video.) Now, this is true, but nothing is perfect. If the signal degradation is too great, errors can be introduced. These error rates can be kept extremely low, but they are still there. In fact, the great success of digital techniques is due just as much to many other factors, such as advances in the fabrication of electronic devices, the integration or 'convergence' of previously separate systems in a common digital form and so on.

Digital computers, however, were not the only 'revolutionary' calculating devices. During the 1920s and 1930s, powerful analogue electromechanical computing machines were developed, particularly at Massachusetts Institute of Technology (MIT) in the United States and Manchester University in the UK (Small, 2001). To begin with, such machines were used to solve problems in such fields as electrical power transmission or the bending of structural beams. Later—and particularly during World War 2 (WW2)—more sophisticated 'differential analyzers' (as they were called) were used in the development of radar, the calculation of shell trajectories for the military and so on. Such computations could take several hours or even longer to set up on what appear now to us as rather clumsy devices— but they would have been infeasible by hand. A related technology was the electronic gun-director, a system for automatically aiming anti-aircraft weapons. As a result of the technological developments of the early 1940s, a very high proportion of the V1s (the so-called 'flying bomb', an early German cruise missile) were shot down in the defence of Antwerp in 1944. The contribution of such devices to the war effort was enormous, yet we hear far more today about early digital computers that were being developed at the same time.

A second and largely independent 'revolution' in analogue computation occurred after WW2, in connection with the control of large-scale industrial processes and guidance systems for aircraft and missiles—two of the most important areas of post-WW2 technology. These new analogue computers exploited high-performance electronic devices that had been developed initially for the telecommunications industry and were key for the design of much Cold War technology such as nuclear reactors and intercontinental missiles. Indeed, for some time there was heated debate as to whether or not they were inferior to the rapidly evolving digital computers. For a long time, definitions of 'computer' referred to the analogue vs. digital debate. For certain problems at least, analogue computers could be much faster. Small (2001) relates in some detail the conflicting claims of analogue and digital computers: for certain simulations of technological systems, analogue computers could certainly be much faster in the 1950s, and even in the 1960s, school students were introduced to the concept of the analogue computer alongside its ever stronger rival, the digital computer. Analogue computers, however, were limited to a much more restricted application area than the newcomer and became an increasingly specialised field.

Electromechanical and electronic devices were not the only means of practical computing before the digital computer finally won out. A largely forgotten, and rather bizarre, device was the Phillips Machine, a hydraulic model of a national economy, used to try to predict economic behaviour in the early 1950s (Bissell, 2007). The flow of money was represented by water flowing through pipes; bank and government reserves were represented by tanks; and valves could be set to represent interest rates and so on.

Digital Computational Revolution?

Jon Agar posed the question: *"what difference did access to computers make to the first generation of scientists to use them?"* (2006, p.869). Agar examines the rhetoric about the use of computers in the natural sciences and questions whether the digital computer really did render previously intractable problems tractable. He notes that quite often computers merely routinised existing techniques, with economic gains with respect to time or personnel, and he argues for a critical stance towards claims such as

> Rapid advances in computer power are leading to completely new ways of doing science. Longstanding problems that were completely intractable by purely experimental methods are now yielding to computational attack.
> (Quoted in Agar, 2006, p.870)

But division of labour certainly became important with the advent of computers, and scientists became increasingly dependent on engineers or computation experts. Agar is quite critical of Douglas Robertson's claim for a "phase change" in science brought about by computers (Robertson, 2003), but he does acknowledge that computers enable a 'new way of seeing'. One rather ironic example of the latter is the way modern engineering software uses elements of older, analogue techniques—not as a method of computation, but as part of the user interface. For example, the powerful computational package MatLab uses an interface that looks very similar to an analogue computer: the user 'connects' the 'devices' on-screen, using a mouse. Similarly, what used to be thought of as out-of-date engineering charts, designed originally to avoid the need for time-consuming calculation, are used to present information to the user in a compact and meaningful way. Another example, more familiar to most readers, is the way that time is often displayed, even when the technology is inherently digital (on a computer or mobile phone screen, for example, or projected onto a wall), using a clock hand.

From these examples we might reasonably conclude that

- what we often call 'revolutionary' technological change is often neither so revolutionary nor so rapid as might appear
- there was an enormously influential 'information technology' even before the development of digital computers
- the element of continuity is often just as important as that of change in the way technology develops

CONCLUSION

A rather sceptical view has been offered in this chapter of 'the information revolution'. But such scepticism does not imply a denial of the *significance* of recent developments. Some of the most important aspects distinguishing recent developments from earlier information and communication technologies are

- the new technologies give users the means to generate, seek, select, obtain, modify and share content on a scale that does seem to be different from earlier technologies
- there are distinct 'postmodern' aspects to this: erosion of authority; the decline of the 'canon' and the 'grand narrative'; a certain 'relativism' (see Weinberger, 2007 for a detailed exploration of related ideas)
- there is a significant blurring of the public and private, both in the use of hardware and in the software of social networking sites—for example, the increasing use of such media as YouTube, Facebook and Twitter by government, educational institutions and private companies
- the danger of the "cult of the amateur" (Keen, 2007), in which the traditional professional expertise of journalists, editors, librarians, academics, etc, is called into question or bypassed

At the beginning of this chapter, I posed a number of questions about 'the information revolution', prompted by Steven Shapin's reading of the Scientific Revolution. I hope to have demonstrated that many of the important questions raised by modern information and communication technologies have been raised before in the context of earlier technologies and still remain unanswered or problematic. I hope, too, that I have demonstrated the complexity of what we call 'the information revolution'. Whatever it is, it is certainly not a "coherent, cataclysmic, and climactic event" (Shapin, 1996, p.1). As to whether it has "fundamentally and irrevocably changed our view of the world" (ibid.) the jury is still out. Despite all the recent hype about ICT, or 'the knowledge economy', and despite all the changes and possibilities brought about by the various new networks and techniques, the basic structures of society are arguably unchanged—it has become something of a truism that the possibilities of e-mail, video conferencing, teleworking, Internet shopping and so on do not seem to have made much of an impact on business travel, international conferences or people travelling daily large distances to work or shop.

However, even given such scepticism about extreme claims for an 'information revolution', it is possible to pick out some real changes of high significance. The Internet, much more than any earlier media technology, is centred on user *demand*. Media products such as newspapers (and their archives), radio and television programmes (and archives), MP3 music files, video, podcasts, etc are available as and when the user wishes. There are still some problems shipping around the huge data files involved, particularly for high-quality video, but there is as yet no slowing down of higher and higher data rates to consumers. Individuals, too, now have much greater opportunities to create and manipulate their own media products—digital photography and video, for example. At the time of writing, the current 'revolutionary' phenomenon is the growth of products such as Facebook, YouTube, Second Life, Twitter and so on. Such software offers user-friendly ways of constructing and maintaining online (possibly multiple) identities. Chandler (1998) has remarked:

> The 'personal home page' is a new genre brought into existence by that branch of the Internet which is known as the World-Wide Web. Personal home pages are online multi-media texts which address the question, 'Who Am I?'. . . . In such sites, what are visibly 'under construction' are not only the pages but the authors themselves.

Chandler was writing before the advent of Facebook and similar, but his remarks are just as pertinent to these newer technologies.

The rise of the blog is another interesting phenomenon that is often claimed to have shifted influence to the individual. A blog might be thought of as a modern version of the centuries-old 'commonplace book' (a notebook in which quotations, poems and other items that strike the author are recorded). A blog is a sort of online equivalent but containing hot links to the items that have attracted the author's attention, as well as the author's comments. Like other webpages, and unlike the commonplace book, it is available as a media product to anyone with a connection to the Internet.

Again, unlike the commonplace book, many blogs allow others to post material. Blogs came to wide public attention at the time of the Iraq War of 2003, when a number of Iraqis used personal blogs to make available detailed and continuously updated information from the heart of the war. On the other hand, the current proliferation of blogs by journalists and pundits, with their tens or hundreds of comments from informed or ill-informed readers alike, does pose the question of whether such technologies really do empower individuals, or whether they simply add to the noise of cyberspace.

Finally, and most recently, the Web has evolved beyond a tool for simple publication or access to information. Web 2.0 has led to the explosion of social networking and the possibility of online collaboration on the creation of new resources by selecting and combining elements of others—so-called 'mashups', for example. Waiting in the wings is Web 3.0—the semantic Web—in which digital resources will be tagged with 'metadata' (information about the information) to enable the relevance, significance and even, in a sense, the meaning of the content to be evaluated by computer software.

In the midst of all the uncertainties one thing seems to be beyond doubt. The 'new' technologies, like the 'old' technologies of steam, electricity, the telegraph, the telephone, the automobile and so on, will continue to evolve in their social context. They will be continuously re-invented by us and our social institutions as we develop and use them. To paraphrase Winston's (1998) closing comment: in retrospect, 'the information revolution' is likely to appear just as revolutionary—and just as non-revolutionary—as steam, electricity, the automobile or nuclear power.

BIBLIOGRAPHY

Agar, J. (2006) 'What Difference Did Computers Make?', *Social Studies of Science*, vol. 36, no. 6, pp.869–907.

Bissell, C.C. (2007) 'The Moniac. A Hydromechanical Analog Computer of the 1950s', *IEEE Control Systems Magazine*, vol. 27, no. 1, pp.59–64.

Borgmann, A. (1999) *Holding on to Reality. The Nature of Information at the Turn of the Millennium*, Chicago, University of Chicago Press.

Brzezinski, Z. (1970) *Between Two Ages: America's Role in the Technetronic Era*, New York, Viking.

Carey, J.W. and Quirk, J.J. (1970) 'The Mythos of the Electronic Revolution', *The American Scholar*, vol. 39, nos. 2 and 3, pp.219–241 and 395–424.

Chandler, D. (1998) 'Personal Home Pages and the Construction of Identities on the Web', http://www.aber.ac.uk/media/Documents/short/webident.html (Accessed 12 July 2010).

Cordes, J. (2000) 'What you should know about knowledge management', http://www.csoonline.com/article/217169/what-you-should-know-about-knowledge-management (Accessed 16 July 2010).

Edgerton, D. (2006) *The Shock of the Old*, London, Profile Books.

Floridi, L. (2010) *Information. A Very Short Introduction*, Oxford, Oxford University Press.

Garvey, M.A. (1852) *The Silent Revolution. Or, the Future Effects of Steam and Electricity upon the Condition of Mankind*, London, William and Frederick Cash.

Gerovitch, S. (2002) *From Newspeak to Cyberspeak*, Cambridge, Massachusetts, MIT Press.

Gregory, D. (1987) 'The Friction of Distance? Information Circulation and the Mails in Early Nineteenth-Century England', *Journal of Historical Geography*, vol. 13, no. 2, pp.130–154.

Jones, C. et al. (2010) 'Networked Learning, the Net Generation and Digital Natives', *Seventh International Conference on Networked Learning*, Aalborg, Denmark, 3–4 May 2010, http://www.networkedlearningconference.org.uk (Accessed 19 June 2010).

Keen, A. (2007) *The Cult of the Amateur*, London: Doubleday.

Kuhn, T. (1962) *The Structure of Scientific Revolutions*, Chicago, University of Chicago Press.

Latour, B. (1999) 'On Recalling ANT', in Law, J. and Hassard, J. (eds.), *Actor Network Theory and After*, Oxford, Blackwell, pp.15–25.

Odlyzko, A. (2000) 'The History of Communications and Its Implications for the Internet', http://www.dtc.umn.edu/~odlyzko/doc/history.communications0.pdf (Accessed 12 July 2010).

Robertson, D.S. (2003) *Phase Change: the Computer Revolution in Science and Mathematics*, Cambridge, Massachusetts, MIT Press.

Roszak, T. (1986) *The Cult of Information*, Cambridge, Lutterworth Press.

Schivelbusch, W. (1986) *The Railway Journey: The Industrialization of Time and Space in the 19th Century*, Berkeley, California, University of California Press.

Shannon, C.E. (1948) 'A Mathematical Theory of Communication', *Bell System Technical Journal*, vol. 27, no. 3, pp.379–423 and no. 4, pp.623–656.

Shapin, S. (1996) *The Scientific Revolution*, Chicago, University of Chicago Press.

Small, J.S. (2001) *The Analogue Alternative*, London, Routledge.

Standage, T. (1998) *The Victorian Internet: The Remarkable Story of the Telegraph and the Nineteenth Century's On-Line Pioneers*, London, Weidenfeld and Nicholson.

Weinberger, D. (2007) *Everything Is Miscellaneous: The Power of the New Digital Disorder*, New York, Times Books.

Winston, B. (1998) *Media, Technology and Society*, London, Routledge.

4   Information, Meaning and Context

David Chapman

INTRODUCTION: FOUNDATIONS OF INFORMATION THEORY

Authors addressing the question of 'what is information' invariably at some point make reference to the work of Claude Shannon. For some it is merely to distance their own concept of information from that of Shannon, but most see the work of Shannon as the beginning of the exploration of 'information' as a concept that can be addressed scientifically. Borgmann (1999), for example, says: "The birth certificate of information as a prominent word and notion is an article published in 1948 by Claude Shannon" (p.9).

Shannon's paper, "A Mathematical Theory of Communication" (Shannon, 1948), in the words of David Mackay "both created the field of information theory and solved most of its fundamental problems" (Mackay, 2003, p.14). First published in the Bell System Technical Journal, it was reproduced, together with a paper by Warren Weaver entitled "Recent contributions to the Mathematical Theory of Communication" (about which I shall have more to say later), in a 1949 book published as *The Mathematical Theory of Communication* (Shannon and Weaver, 1949).

That *The Mathematical Theory of Communication* is still in print today is one piece of evidence for the far-reaching consequences of Shannon's work, but more dramatic evidence can be seen from how the work has been cited. A search in 2010 using the citation database *Web of Science* revealed more than 7700 documents that cited the 1948 paper, and more were appearing at the rate of around 500 a year. Shannon was working in the telecommunications industry, so it is not surprising that the bulk of the citations come from the disciplines of engineering or computer science but more intriguing are the publications citing Shannon that come from disciplines as diverse as ethics, archaeology, sport sciences and art. In all, *Web of Science* finds citations in publications from more than 200 different subject areas, according to their classification scheme.

In this chapter I summarise some of the key results of Shannon's paper and use ways of thinking derived from more recent work on telecommunications, in order to explore how Shannon's insights might be applied to "the general problem of communication" (to use the terminology of Weaver, 1949, p.97).

OUTLINE OF SHANNON'S THEORY

For Shannon, communication was about conveying a sequence of messages from an information source to a destination (Figure 4.1).

The information source has a set of possible messages to send to the destination. On any given occasion, it selects *one* of these possible messages, and the message is encoded by a transmitter to make the signal, which is sent over the channel and decoded by a receiver, thus recovering the message. On the way through the channel, the signal might become degraded leading to the possibility that the receiver can't decode it correctly. Shannon modelled the degradation by the addition of 'noise' to the signal, and I'll be discussing that in more detail later.

The Shannon-Hartley Definition of Information

A key feature of Shannon's model is the way in which he separates the information from the coding. To understand Shannon's concept of information, we first need to consider what constitutes a message.

The simplest message is the answer to a question which has just two possible answers: yes or no, up or down, win or lose, boy or girl. As used by Shannon (building on work by Hartley, 1928; Nyquist, 1924; 1928), information is measured with units of bits ('information bits', which are related to, but not that same thing as, binary digits). These information bits are calculated such that an answer to a binary question contains 1 bit of information. So, each time a baby is born, 1 bit of information is needed to convey the gender. This could be represented by a binary digit as used by computers, with, say, a '0' meaning a boy and '1' meaning a girl.

If the choice is between more than two options, the information conveyed can be more than 1 bit. Suppose, for example, a hospital has a coding

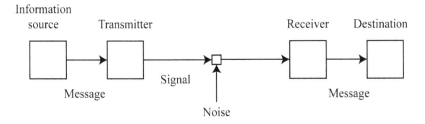

Figure 4.1   Model of communication (after Shannon, 1948).

scheme for the health of the babies born and that they use four categories: green meaning 'healthy', yellow meaning 'some cause for concern', orange meaning 'needs medical attention' and red meaning 'emergency'. With binary digits this might be represented by a pair of digits, say 00 for green; 01 for yellow; 10 for orange and 11 for red.

It is not necessarily the case, however, that the health information is worth two information bits. In terms of Shannon information, the amount of information in a message is determined by the probability of the message (the probability of the answer to the question). If the four categories were all equally probable, they would indeed all be worth 2 bits of information, but that is not how it is here—babies needing emergency treatment are much less common than healthy babies. In general terms, Shannon's analysis determines that less-probable messages convey more information than more probably messages. This means that a message saying a baby needs emergency treatment conveys more information than a message saying a baby is healthy, which is in some ways reasonable because the hospital will carry on with its normal business when the healthy baby is born but will have to spring into action in response to a baby needing emergency treatment. The rare event has a bigger impact. The parents, of course, might have a different perspective: the fact that their baby is healthy is big news to them, even if it is the same news that most other parents get.

Shannon (based on the work of Hartley and others) quantified the information content of a message using a logarithmic measure, and although the details are not important here, it is useful to illustrate his work with some numbers. The specific formula is

$$I_k = -\log_2(p_k)$$

Here, a message that occurs with probability p_k delivers information I_k. With two equally probable messages, like the example of 'boy' or 'girl', each message has probability of ½. Putting this into the formula, we see that $I = -\log_2(0.5) = 1$, giving the result we used earlier that a message about the gender of baby is worth 1 bit of information. With four equally probable messages, each message has a probability of ¼, and $I = -\log_2(0.25) = 2$, again agreeing with what we saw earlier. Suppose, to illustrate the calculation, that the probabilities of the health messages comes out as 80% for green (eight out of ten babies are healthy), 15% yellow, 4% orange and 1% red. These probabilities translate to 0.32 bits of information from a green message, 2.74 from a yellow, 4.64 from an orange and 6.64 from a red message. The point to notice here is that whereas with four equally probable messages each message delivers 2 bits of information, in this case one message, the most common message, delivers rather less than 2 bits (less than 1 bit in fact) while the other messages deliver more than 2 bits.

For Shannon's purposes, in analysing a communications channel, the information value of a single instance of a message was not what was important. Shannon envisaged a channel sending a sequence of such messages: some one answer, some another, and what was important for the analysis was the average information per message. Over a long enough time, all possible messages would be sent, but they would occur with different frequencies, depending upon their relative probabilities. Messages from a hospital about the gender of the babies born there are relatively straightforward, since the probability of a boy or a girl are roughly equal, each ½, so there will be approximately as many messages saying 'boy' as 'girl' (that is to say, in this case the relative frequencies of the different messages do *not* vary). Furthermore, each message, as we saw before, carries 1 bit of information, so the average information per message is also 1 bit per message.

With the health messages, most will be the green messages, delivering 0.32 bits of information, but some will be delivering more, and if you do the calculation, it comes out with an average of 0.92 bits per message. If the four messages had occurred with equal probability, they would all have delivered 2 bits, and the average would have been 2 bits per message.

The average information per message is an important parameter in Shannon's analysis and was called by Shannon the *entropy* of the source.

Shannon's Noisy Channel Coding Theorem

Having established a quantifiable measure of information, Shannon was then able to derive a formula for the rate at which this information can be sent over a communication channel. Specifically, he derived his famous formula for the capacity of a noisy communication channel:

$$C = B \log_2(1+S/N)$$

Understanding the mathematics is not important, but what is important is that a number, C, can be calculated for the channel capacity, measured in information bits per second. This could be, for example, 10 bits per second or 1 kbit/s (kilobit per second which is 1000 bits per second). The formula shows how you can calculate information capacity from the physical parameters of the channel, using knowledge of the bandwidth of the channel (B), the power being used to transmit the signal (S) and the power of the interfering noise (N).

To those without a technical background, these parameters, B, S and N, might seem mysterious, but the important thing to appreciate is that they are all physical properties of the channel: they can all be measured with test equipment. S and N are powers which could be measured in units of Watts, just like power needed to run a vacuum cleaner or a kettle. The channel bandwidth, B, is the range of frequencies that can be sent through the channel. The idea of frequency is less of an everyday concept than power but is encountered in the context of analogue radios, where you tune to different stations by selecting different frequencies. The range of different frequencies that you can select on the radio—the range over which you can tune it—is the bandwidth of the radio.

Shannon's achievement was to show how knowledge of these physical parameters of a communications channel can be used to determine the maximum theoretical capacity of the channel and shows the trade-off between different parameters. Calculation of the capacity of a communications channel is a fundamental underlying theory to the work of all communications engineering, and indirectly to the achievements of 'information age'. Whenever we connect to the Internet or use our mobile phones, we are making use of communication channels which have been engineered to carry as much information as possible. Shannon's formula tells us what is possible, what can't be done, and what needs to be changed to get more capacity.

There has been a lot of debate about the relationship between Shannon's 'information' and other concepts of information—indeed this book is part of the ongoing debate. Shannon's formula for the capacity of a noise channel seems to be making a link between two very different categories of things: material, physical things like signal powers and something rather less physical, which Shannon called 'information'. Some people have objected even to the use of the word information in this context or at least insist on a qualifier such as 'selective information'. Whatever word or phrase is used, however, there is something intriguing about what the equation brings together. Remember that these are selections or choices among alternatives. If the channel capacity is calculated to be, say, 100 bits per second, we can convey the equivalent of 100 binary decisions every second. This surely is taking us closer to the realm of thoughts and ideas, things that are legitimately classed as information, than the world of matter and energy.

Later in this chapter, I shall explore ways in which we might move from Shannon's information to broader concepts of information through the use of the layering metaphor of engineering, but first I want to digress briefly with a story that emphasises the remarkable significance of Shannon's equation, even just in terms of engineering.

Turbo Coding and the Limits to Channel Capacity

Knowing the theoretical channel capacity is only the first step for the communications engineer. Shannon's work allowed engineers to determine the theoretical maximum capacity, but engineering a real system to achieve that maximum is a different matter. The key, as Shannon himself showed, is in the design of the encoding and decoding.

As I said earlier, the effect of noise on the channel is that the messages might not arrive correctly. Consider communicating the message 'boy' or 'girl' from the maternity unit. The simplest coding over a digital communication channel for this would be, for example, to use a binary '0' to mean a boy and a '1' to mean a girl. On one occasion a message saying that the child was a girl, sent using the sign '1', might get corrupted and received as a '0' with the result that the destination thinks that a boy was born. Better coding can reduce the chance of this happening. So, for example, the sign used for a girl could be three 1s (111) and for a boy three 0s (000). Now if one of the 1s in the girl's sign is received as a 0, the decoder gets, say, 101 instead of 111. Although this is wrong, it is more like the sign for a girl than the sign for a boy, so it is correctly decoded to mean girl. This is an example of a repetition code—you just repeat '1' three times for a girl and repeat '0' three times for a boy.

With very simple codes, we find that in practice we cannot get very close to the channel capacity. If Shannon's formula suggests that the capacity is, say, 1000 bits per second, we might find that in practice we only send as few as 10 bits per second. If we try to send more, too many of them get corrupted.

There are much more sophisticated codes that can be used, however, and by using better codes, we can get closer to the limit given by Shannon's formula. Nevertheless, for almost fifty years, it proved impossible to approach the Shannon limit very closely, and there seemed a practical limit that was rather less than Shannon's.

All that changed in 1993 when three researchers from France presented a conference paper (Berrou et al., 1993) which described a coding technique which they called "turbo coding", that they claimed almost achieved the Shannon limit. So remarkable was this claim, that the first time a paper was submitted, it was rejected as being too good to be true (Burr, 2001)! Since then turbo codes and other related techniques have become widely used, and Shannon-limit performance is no longer pure theory.

LAYERED ARCHITECTURES

A number of authors have addressed the bridge between the technology of a communications link and human communication by invoking layering metaphors. Warren Weaver did this in his article that appeared alongside Shannon's paper in the 1949 book, talking of three levels corresponding to what he referred to as the technical problem (level A), the semantic problem (level B) and the effectiveness problem (level C). These three levels roughly corresponded to the levels that Colin Cherry discussed in his 1957 book *On Human Communication* (Cherry, 1957). Cherry drew from the field of semiotics and identified layers that address syntactics, semantics and pragmatics. Although Cherry drew a distinction between his layers and those of Weaver, they were, broadly speaking, taking a similar approach, with the bottom layer (technical/syntactics) being where the work of Shannon applies, the semantic level being where we start to talk about meaning and the top level (effectiveness/pragmatics) where we consider the impact on people.

In this chapter, however, I come to layering from a slightly different direction, drawing on the way in which layered metaphors have been used in engineering (see, for example, standard texts on data communications such as Tannenbaum, 2002; Stallings, 2010).

In Figure 4.2, I have redrawn Figure 4.1 to show layering.

Within the metaphor, the encoding and decoding take place 'below' the information source and destination. This vertical relationship is indicated by the positioning of the transmitter and receiver on the diagram, and in Figure 4.2, I am also using the convention of drawing the boxes for the encoding and decoding as trapeziums. A feature of this layered metaphor is that we talk about 'virtual communication' taking place at higher levels, which is shown on the diagram with a dashed line (a 'virtual channel'). So there is a virtual communication channel for the message, while the physical communication takes places at the lower level.

For example, suppose the message is a colour, and that we are communicating a selection from the four possible colours of green, yellow, orange and red. Suppose further that on one particular occasion the message is yellow. This, 'yellow', is what is conveyed over the virtual channel, while the transmitter might code it as 01, which is what is carried over the physical channel.

The idea of layers introduces a new dimension to the communication, and we can extend up and down to bring in more aspects of the communication, which is what has been done in Figure 4.3. 'Downwards', the 01 that I previously called the signal, would have some physical representation. It might be pulses of light in an optical fibre, or it might be a radio

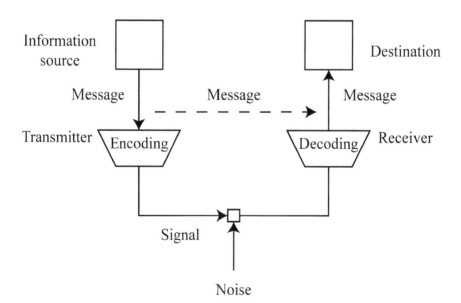

Figure 4.2   Model of communication, redrawn to emphasise layers.

signal. The process of generating a physical signal we call modulation, and detection of the physical signal is demodulation, so we have the modulation/demodulation layer below the binary data.

Extending upwards takes in what the colours 'mean'. Using the example from earlier—the health of newborn babies—yellow means 'some cause for concern'. The virtual channel at the top is now the state of health of the baby; this is colour coded in the layer below and then digitally coded in the next layer before the modulation.

Within the context of communication systems engineering, standardised layered architectures have been defined, such as the seven-layer model for Open Systems Interconnection (the 'OSI model') and the 'TCP/IP protocols' of the Internet. (The Transmission Control Protocol, TCP, is at a level above the Internet Protocol, IP. Likewise, the Hypertext Transfer Protocol, HTTP, familiar from webpage addresses, is at a level above TCP. The details of these protocols are not relevant for the present discussion.) For some purposes, working within a standardised framework is important—it allows equipment constructed by different manufacturers to work together, for example (that was the meaning of the word 'open' in 'Open Systems Interconnection'). However, the way of thinking in terms of layers permeates the design of many engineered systems and not just communication

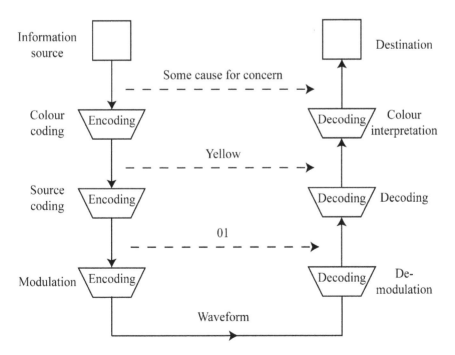

Figure 4.3   Further layers in a communication channel.

systems. It is that way of thinking and some of the conventions used in engineering that I want to draw upon while working towards some insights into the nature of information.

The Search for Meaning

Looking back to Figure 4.3 and specifically at moving up the stack on the right-hand side, notice how we get successive levels of meaning. The physical signal is taken to mean the binary bits 01. The binary 01 is taken to mean yellow, and yellow is taken to mean 'some cause for concern'.

Shannon, however, in his 1948 paper, was careful to distance himself from any talk of 'meaning':

> Frequently the messages have meaning; that is they refer to or are correlated according to some system with certain physical or conceptual entities. These semantic aspects of communication are irrelevant to the engineering problem. (Shannon, 1948, p.379)

Warren Weaver, in his paper, "Some recent contributions to the mathematical theory of communication" which was published alongside Shannon's 1948 paper in the 1949 book (Shannon and Weaver, 1949) commented on that statement of Shannon's:

> But this does not mean that the engineering aspects are necessarily irrelevant to the semantic aspects. (Weaver, 1949, pp.99–100)

The problem seems to be the distance between a purely physical (material/mechanical) mechanism—sound waves in the air, voltage on a wire, light level in an optical fibre or the amount of ink the page, for that matter—and a meaningful concept in the brain of a human being. Donald Mackay, speaking on BBC radio in 1960, put it like this:

> The original speaker, we may suppose, means something by what he says . . . yet in the next stages . . . (the generation of sound waves and all the rest of it) all signs of his meaning seem to have disappeared. Discussion at this level proceeds in exactly the same terms whether the air is handling the outpourings of a genius of the jabber of a monkey. Yet finally, when the message reaches the ear of the human listener, its 'meaning' seems to pop up again from nowhere . . . There are in fact two awkward discontinuities in this way of telling the story: a jump from meaningful utterance to meaningless air vibrations; and then back again. (Mackay, 1969, p.20)

Mackay went on to address the problem in terms of the selective function of messages on "the state of conditional readiness for behaviour" of the brain and argued that "this opposition of 'meaningful' and 'mechanical' is false" (Mackay, 1969, p.21).

Expressed in the way that I did at the beginning of this section (the physical signal means the binary bits 01, 01 means yellow, and yellow means 'some cause for concern'); however, it seemed quite painless to move from the physical signal all the way up to the very human concept of 'some cause for concern', with no apparent awkward discontinuities. Maybe if there is a discontinuity, it is right at the bottom where material is used to carry 'Shannon information', and the discontinuity is bridged by Shannon's equation for the capacity of a noisy channel, as I discussed earlier. Above that, we have entered the realm of information and left the material world behind.

We need to be careful, though, because the concept of 'meaning' is not straightforward. Saying that something 'means' something else is open to various interpretations. The usage here is, broadly speaking, a semiotic usage, which I shall be looking at a little more later. First, I want to explore some more trapeziums.

More Layers

The system for reporting the health of babies was artificial, presented to illustrate some aspects of Shannon's communication model. Figure 4.4 looks at a more realistic example of communication, in which one person

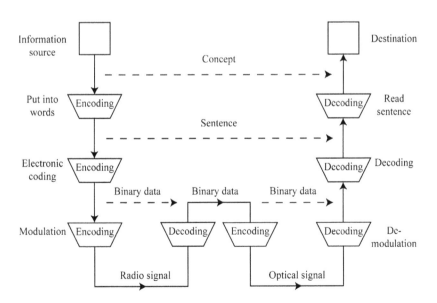

Figure 4.4   More advanced use of layers in communication.

(the originator) communicates with another person (the recipient), using text carried over a telecommunications system.

The originator has some concept to convey to the recipient, which they do by putting the concept into words which are then digitally encoded and modulated for transmission. At the destination, the physical signal is demodulated to recover the digital data, which is then decoded to get the words of the sentence. The sentence is read and interpreted by the recipient to extract the concept. 'Concepts' are, of course, much more complex things than words or binary digits, but that does not invalidate the layered model. The complexity of the concept is dealt with in the appropriate layer.

Figure 4.4 assumes that on the way from the source to the destination, two different transmission media are used. First the signal is carried over a wireless (radio) link, then further on, it uses an optical fibre. Because different modulation systems are needed for the different media, the signal is demodulated back to the binary data and modulated again for the new medium, which can be seen in the middle of the diagram. This intermediate stage which shows decoding and recoding without going all the way up the 'stack' again illustrates a way of thinking drawn from engineering, which can provide insights for the general problem of communication.

Semiotics

It is not appropriate, nor is there space, to explore semiotics in depth here, but there are a few basic ideas that we can exploit to extract further insights into the communication process as modelled by the layered diagrams.

Signs are modelled in different ways in different semiotic traditions, but the most basic is the dyadic, two-part, model of Ferdinand de Saussure (1974). In this model (discussed by Chandler, 2002), a sign consists of the signified (the concept) and the signifier (the representation). This distinction is illustrated in Figure 4.5a.

Note that the sign is the combination of these two: the signifier alone does not constitute the sign. For Saussure both the signifier and the signified were psychological, although later usage has sometimes interpreted the signifier as the physical form of the sign. Roland Barthes (1957) gives the example of a bunch of roses (the signifier) to signify a suitor's passion (the signified). The bunch of roses signifying passion constitutes the sign.

I want to suggest a parallel between a semiotic sign and the trapeziums of Figures 4.2, 4.3 and 4.4. At the bottom of the trapezium is the signifier, at the top, the signified. For example, in the American Standard Code for Information Interchange (ASCII) the bits '01100001' (the signifier) signifies the letter 'a', as shown in Figure 4.5b. In Figure 4.5c, I have introduced another interpretation, building in the idea that 0110001 'means' the letter 'a', so I am suggesting that the trapezium links the 'data' to the 'meaning'. Or, maybe the 'meaning' of the data is the 'information'—which fits with

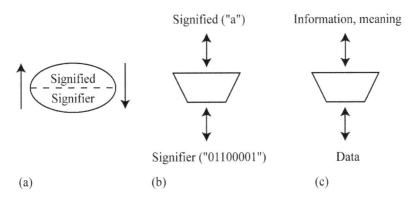

Figure 4.5   (a) Saussure's model of a sign, (b) as a trapezium, (c) the relationship between data and meaning.

the definition quoted by Bissell in Chapter 3 that information is comprised of data in context.

Alternative semiotic models of a sign are triadic and illustrated by triangles similar to that of Figure 4.6a. There are many variations, but, broadly speaking, they extend the dyadic model by introducing explicit consideration of the process of interpretation of the sign. Thus, the bits '01100001' only signify the letter 'a' in a context where they are being used as an ASCII code, in the same way that a bunch of roses only signify passion when used for that purpose.

In Figure 4.6a, I have chosen a variation which suits my purposes, although not matching any of the standard semiotic triangles such as Peirce's 'representamen, interpretant and object' (Hartshorne and Weiss, 1965) or Ogden and Richards' 'symbol, thought or reference and referent' (Ogden and Richards, 1949).

With trapeziums the interpreter is readily identified with activity of the trapezium itself, the encoder/decoder or the context, as shown in Figures 4.6b and 4.6c.

Whether or not we can legitimately suggest that the encoding and/or decoding of a message 'is' a sign, the parallel helps the reading of the trapezium diagrams and provides some useful insights. In particular, an important insight of semiotics is that signs are meaningless in isolation: they only have meaning in relation to other signs. This is true of the trapeziums too. Binary data—a string of 1s and 0s—are completely meaningless without the context. In Figure 4.4, the trapezium can only decode the binary data into a sentence using a programme that reads binary data as text.

Each layer in the diagram corresponds to a sign-system. There is meaning *within* each layer by virtue of the relations between the signs within that layer, but trying to find the meaning from one layer within another layer is

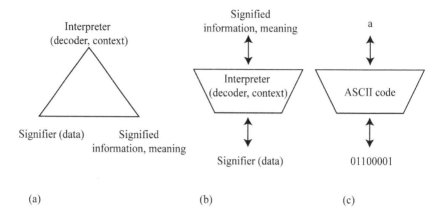

Figure 4.6   (a) A semiotic triangle, (b) encoding/decoding as triadic sign, (c) ASCII code as a sign.

fruitless. It is akin to trying to find the concept of passion within the biology of roses—a kind of reductionism. The meaning of the letter 'a' cannot be found in the digits 01100001, and the meaning of the word 'war' cannot be found in the letters 'w', 'a' and 'r'. Notice that this definition of 'meaning' (information) is relative rather than absolute. Meaning emerges at the layer boundaries, but the meaning is only relative to the layer below.

It is important to appreciate, however, what is and what is not implied by the 'independence' of layers. Meaning does not transfer between layers as we have seen, but the capabilities of a layer have an impact on the layer above in terms of the service that it can deliver. Also, it was Weaver's contention that "the mathematical theory of communication . . . although ostensibly applicable only to level A [technical] problems, actually is helpful and suggestive for level B [semantic] and level C [effectiveness] problems" (Weaver, 1949, p.114).

An example of that is the discovery of Hartley and Shannon of the relationship between probability and information content: low probability of a message corresponds to high information content. This was important for the technicalities of data communication systems, but it is an idea that works at other levels too. The answer 'yes' to the question 'have I won the lottery' provides me with more information than 'no', but 'winning the lottery' is a high-level concept and a long way from the technical details of a communications link.

CONCLUSIONS

This chapter has brought together ideas from semiotics and the layered architectures of engineering in order to provide a framework that bridges the gap between communications technology and human communication. It has suggested that the concept of information as introduced by Hartley and Shannon is essentially of the same substance as the semantic information of semiologists, but that Shannon was addressing information at the lowest level in a layered hierarchy whereas semiotics is concerned with the higher levels where information interacts with the human mind.

The framework is essentially a re-working of the ideas proposed by Weaver and by Cherry, and provides a means of dividing up 'the general problem of communication' into coherent fields that can be analysed in isolation from each other. In this chapter we have seen how Shannon analysed one level in detail in his classic paper of 1948, and work on that level continues in the developments of computer and communications technologies to this day. We saw earlier in this chapter, for example, the extraordinary story of the development of turbo codes in the 1990s.

Other chapters in this book explore information at higher levels. Chapter 9 by Piwek, for example, explores information in the context of human conversations. Piwek is not interested in the digital coding or the physical representation of the words and sentences because his chapter is exploring information at a higher level than that addressed by Shannon. Chapter 11 by Corrigan with its focus on information laws and intellectual property is arguably at an even higher level.

At the end of his chapter in *The Mathematical Theory of Communication*, Weaver suggested of Shannon's work:

> [T]his analysis has so penetratingly cleared the air that one is now, perhaps for the first time, ready for a real theory of meaning. (Weaver, 1949, p.116)

Through the use of a definition of meaning based on an interpretation of the meaning of semiotic signs, this chapter has described a way of talking about meaning that can be applied at all levels of the general problem of communication.

BIBLIOGRAPHY

Barthes, R. (1957) *Mythologies*, translated by Annette Lavers 2009, London, Vintage Classics.

Berrou, C., Glavieux, A. and Thitimajshima, P. (1993) 'Near Shannon Limit Error-Correcting Coding and Decoding: Turbo-Codes', in *Proceedings of the IEEE International Conference on Communications (ICC 93)*, Geneva, 23–26 May 1993, pp.1064–1070.

Borgmann, A. (1999) *Holding on to Reality: The Nature of Information at the Turn of the Millennium*, Chicago, University of Chicago Press.

Burr, A.G. (2001) 'Turbo-Codes: The Ultimate Error Control Codes?', *IEE Electronics and Communication Engineering Journal,* vol. 13, no. 4, pp.155–165.

Chandler, D. (2002) *Semiotics: The Basics*, London, Routledge.

Cherry, C. (1957) *On Human Communication*, Cambridge, Massachusetts, MIT Press.

de Saussure, F. (1974) *Course in General Linguistics*, London, Peter Owen.

Hartley, R. (1928) 'Transmission of Information', *Bell System Technical Journal*, vol. 7, no. 3, pp.535–563.

Hartshorne, C. and Weiss, P., eds. (1965) *Collected Papers of Charles Sanders Peirce, Volume I: Principles of Philosophy and Volume II: Elements of Logic*, Cambridge, Massachusetts, The Belknap Press of Harvard University Press.

Mackay, D. (1969) *Information, Mechanism and Meaning*, Cambridge, Massachusetts, MIT Press.

Mackay, D.J.C. (2003) *Information Theory, Inference, and Learning Algorithms*, Cambridge, United Kingdom, Cambridge University Press.

Nyquist, H. (1924) 'Certain Factors Affecting Telegraph Speed', *Transactions of the American Institute of Electrical Engineers*, vol. 43, pp.412–422.

Nyquist, H. (1928) 'Certain Topics in Telegraph Transmission Theory', *Transactions of the American Institute of Electrical Engineers*, vol. 47, no. 2, pp.617–644.

Ogden, C.K. and Richards, I.A. (1949) *The Meaning of Meaning*, 10th ed., London, Routledge and Kegan Paul.

Shannon, C.E. (1948) 'A Mathematical Theory of Communication', *Bell System Technical Journal*, vol. 27, no. 3, pp.379–423 and no. 4, pp.623–656.

Shannon, C.E. and Weaver, W. (1949) *The Mathematical Theory of Communication*, Urbana, University of Illinois Press.

Stallings, W. (2010) *Data and Computer Communications*, 9th ed., Upper Saddle River, New Jersey, Pearson Prentice Hall.

Tannenbaum, A.S. (2002) *Computer Networks*, 4th ed., Upper Saddle River, New Jersey, Pearson Education.

Weaver, W. (1949) 'Recent Contributions to the Mathematical Theory of Communication', in Shannon, C.E. and Weaver, W. (eds.) *The Mathematical Theory of Communication*, Urbana, University of Illinois Press, pp.93–117.

5 Signs and Signals

John Monk

METAPHOR, ANALOGY AND SIGNS

Ralph Hartley, a pioneer of Information Theory, declared, "Information is a very elastic term" (Hartley, 1928), and although Information Theory is rooted in probabilities, a statistician observed, "The key word in Statistics is information. . . . But, what is information? No other concept in statistics is more elusive in its meaning and less amenable to a generally agreed definition" (Basu, 1975).

We say we have information but can only offer indirect evidence. Information is referred to metaphorically using words like 'carrying' and 'conveying' which treat information as a substance that forms, for instance, scraps, pieces or nuggets and is "'processed,' 'stored,' 'retrieved,' 'compressed,' 'chopped,' etc., as if it were hamburger meat" (von Foerster, 1970, p.30).

Klaus Krippendorf (1993) listed ways of talking about communicating information. Developments in rapidly changing fields like the telephone, he suggested, encouraged the use of metaphor and the import of "suitable explanatory structures". Information as a fluid is a common metaphor; for instance, it was reported that a politician "swamped the war party by the deluge of information . . . which he poured upon the table" (Anonymous, 1844), but in his speech in Edinburgh, a Mr Macauly announced, "We take knowledge to be the mind's digestion of information" (Anonymous, 1846; Anonymous, 1847). Like the metaphors, the verb 'to inform' suggests a transfer to someone whereas 'to know' requires a "knower" (Brown and Duguid, 2002, p.120) so that knowledge is embodied while information may not be.

I am informed when I find out something about the state of the world, perhaps when I feel the rain, or maybe discover something about people's beliefs, expectations or intentions, for example, the railway employees' intentions to secure the arrival of a train at the time printed in the timetable. Or I might learn of people's wishes expressed, for instance, on a sign that says, *"Please shut the gate"*.

That is when I say I am dealing with information I am most likely dealing with signs—artefacts, objects or declarations—fragments of a discourse that provide me with clues that reduce my uncertainty about what I might do and what might happen.

Some signs once installed remain unaltered; they inform, become familiar and posit nothing new, a statue of some long deceased politician, for example (Kruk, 2010); though sometimes what they acclaim changes as the political climate alters. Other physical signs inform us of something changeable, for example, the screens of dealers that display commodity prices. Then there are the hybrids, messages that scroll across public displays, changing moment by moment but repeating after a time. Similarly lighthouses identify themselves with a sequence of intervals of light and dark repeated to reflect an unchanging identity. Where the physical sign changes, the term 'signal' is sometimes used. Railway signals, for example, report on the current occupation of the track ahead which will change.

INFORMATION NEEDS PEOPLE

Fisher explained, statisticians take data, which "by its mere bulk is incapable of entering the mind", and replace it with fewer quantities that "contain as much as possible . . . of the relevant information contained in the original data" and exclude "irrelevant information" (Fisher, 1922). This implies statistical methods have inbuilt criteria for separating irrelevant from relevant information which was inefficiently expressed in the 'data', and since relevancy is relative to a purpose, dealing with information is a human task. This view is reinforced by an article attempting to answer the question "What is information?"; the authors explain, "The word 'Information' derives from human intercourse" therefore the term 'information' in other contexts is used in an "anthropomorphic sense" (Engelberg and Boyarsky, 1979, p. 318). One example they offer involves the hormone thyotropin, which is produced in the pituitary and affects the thyroid's production of an iodine-rich hormone. It could be said that thyotropin 'contains information' that 'instructs' the thyroid gland. The use of the word 'instructs' makes the system components sound like a teacher and a student and suggests a causal connection that channels attention towards a purpose: thyroxin production. Two criteria emerge: first, information is associated with a function or purpose; second, 'informational' relationships are causal.

Edison's original phonograph created a wiggly impression on tin foil, an analogue of sound, which was replayed on a particular type of machine. The trace on the foil was analogous to the sound, though the replayed sound was a distorted and noisy version of the original and a "perceptible loss was found . . . in the quality of the utterance" (Edison, 1878). The properties of the analogue enabled sound to be treated differently: the analogue was persistent and transportable allowing the reproduction of the sound at different times and possibly different places. If the original speech was informative, then the recorded speech had the potential to be informative when replayed. So information is 'carried' by a phenomenon or object when it is potentially a link in a causal chain that ultimately informs someone. This can only be claimed if the original was informative, the causal links are dependable and there is an instrument that will create an intelligible transcription.

MATERIALITY

Michel Foucault (1994) wrote about discourse—roughly a collection of related conversations and documents confined to a social institution. Foucault's work focussed on documents containing text, lists, tables and so on, but his perspective is germane to other kinds of signs. According to Foucault, the components of discourse are statements composed of one or more juxtaposed signs that may be transmitted, preserved, attributed value, repeated, reproduced or transformed. Hence a statement requires a technology to transform it across time and across space and thus "a material existence . . . even if it is doomed to vanish as soon as it appears" (Foucault, 1994, p.100). Each statement and therefore each sign are coupled with a specific material institution that produces, processes and, potentially, destroys signs. Such institutions include radio broadcasting, sign writing, money minting, the Mafia, education, social networking, fashion, advertising or packaging.

Materiality implies "a statement must have a substance, a support, a place, and a date" (Foucault, 1994, p.101) each of which are constituents of the statement. For example, precious metals are parts of statements made by artefacts such as wedding rings and regal crowns. Changing aspects of a sign can change the identity of the statement it makes. For instance, whenever a sign is copied or encountered at a different time or in a different place, it makes a different statement (Foucault, 1994, p.101). Modifications to the way a sign is supported are unlikely to affect the statement it makes. Nevertheless, material signs commonly need infrastructures, perhaps provided by a simple pole to support the sign, illumination, an electrical power supply or the pulleys, ropes and masts for raising nautical flags.

Saussure studied speech and developed a theory that, he envisaged, would create a "science that studies the life of signs within society" (de Saussure, 1959, p.16). He supposed signs have two aspects: one, the signifier, related to the physical sign and the other, the signified, a concept. The association between the two is arbitrary but held in place by accustomed use. An illustration of the strength and flimsiness of the connection occurs in the play, William Tell; first a tyrannical governor orders passing burghers to salute a hat, which is set upon a pole erected in the town square and which symbolises the occupying power. Later the citizens overthrow the governor but still see the hat as a source of power and cry "Into the fire with it." But a voice announces, "No! Preserve it! It had to be the tool of tyranny now it will be a sign of Freedom!" (von Schiller, 2005). The hat, the signifier, instantly became associated with a new signified as the result of the new resolution.

The arbitrariness of the connection between signifier and signified gives sign-makers latitude in choosing signifiers that meet particular practical requirements. A sign must stand out and must therefore be perceptible hence stock exchange traders, tic-tac men at the racecourse signalling odds and cricket umpires choose sign language rather than speech to overcome distance and the noise surrounding them in their work (Scroggie, 2008).

The material might propagate the sign or signal overland or perpetuate the sign; the sign may be required to operate underwater, show up at night, conserve energy or be easy to make. Obviously signs should withstand the conditions they are exposed to. The material for a war memorial, for example, should be durable.

Spoken linguistic signs do not need special hardware and most people, after their apprenticeship, converse unaided, but the product is transient. Other physical signs employ technological aids to extend the range of expression. Some are simple like the squeeze of a rubber bulb of a hooter or the press of a button to sound a doorbell. Writing demands greater skill and produces enduring records but requires implements such as pencils and paper or keyboards and screens. Some modes of expression, for instance, television commercials, employ teams of people in the design, production, presentation and, possibly, maintenance of signs that cannot be deployed spontaneously. And production can be a side effect of other activities, for example, in Soviet Estonia, by decree the regime destroyed land ownership patterns, but recent land reforms treated "old boundary stones, trees and stone walls" and continued customary farming and social activities as signs defining boundaries (Maandi, 2009).

A consequence of the materiality is that a sign has to compete with other material objects for space, time and attention and can intrude on or interfere with other material objects. Signs are ineffective when they are not recognised as signs. They can be imperceptible because they are out of range, generate only feeble effects, masked by other phenomena or objects or do not match the observer's skills or capabilities. And a sign can be confusing when it is difficult to differentiate from other signs. Crucially a sign must be perceptible, intelligible and distinctive.

Distinction can be provided by modulating the material substrate of a sign, for instance by shaping, colouring or adding text. A sign at Kouchibouguac has four painted coloured patches corresponding to different levels of fire hazard and an arrow picks out the patch that indicates the current state of the forest, and tram drivers in Antwerp respond to traffic lights displaying an alphabet of distinctive illuminated circles and oblongs at different angles. Time is a dimension providing the identifying intervals of occultation and illumination of a navigation light. The flags locating holes in golf offer an example of a system with a binary distinction. The system is one of difference since a flag indicates a hole and no flag indicates there is no hole (Royal and Ancient, 2010).

GAMES

Strings of binary digits encode the diversity of data processed by digital systems, so a definition of the significance of a single bit would result in a list describing all possible uses of a bit. Similarly a dictionary lists all the possible uses of each word. Ludwig Wittgenstein, aware of the variety of ways words were used and the possible alternative ways in which things could be expressed introduced the phrase "language games", for those linguistic practices where we do things with words; amongst his examples were giving orders, describing an appearance, speculating about an event, solving an arithmetic problem and making up a story (Wittgenstein, 1992, §23). Wittgenstein chooses the term games, not to trivialise language uses, but to point out they appear to have rules borne of habit. Additionally within a game, players are free to choose their moves, so developing a skill to find the best moves is worthwhile, and games can involve any number of players, depending on the rules of the game. Effectively a language game contextualises words and focusses on linguistic tasks. By extension it becomes possible to talk about sign games.

For example, I can put two things side by side and compare their heights. Or it might be more convenient to mark a stick with the height of one object and take the stick to the other object and check it against the mark. In this instance the marked stick is a sign of height and might be said to hold information about the height of a particular object. However, the stick is not essential in performing a comparison but is instrumental in one particular technique, or sign game.

Paraphrasing Saussure's account, sign use is a social phenomenon relying on widespread usage and general acceptance (de Saussure, 1959, p.67). The utility of signs arises because users in a particular sign-rich institution acquire similar habits and recognise those habits in others (de Saussure, 1959, p.14) to become competent players of the institution's sign games. Effectively, observation and practice in the use of copies provide the apprenticeship for individuals who learn the functioning of signs (de Saussure, 1959, p.14). Over time habits and games change, but individuals cannot force the adoption of new habits, and sign games necessitating heavy investment in material components, training and infrastructures will face cultural, economic and environmental constraints that forestall changes.

Physics enters in to limit our capacity to act and react not so much in terms of strength but in terms of our sluggishness. Personal limitations restrict the number of games anyone can join, and we are likely to have a greater fluency within some games than in others; nevertheless, people will engage in a number of sign games and must expect them to interfere with one another since occasionally attention to one demands neglect of another or the materiality of the signs of one game obscures the signs of another.

THEORY

A number of authors identify a variety of functions all signs, or messages, perform. Shannon, who "put information theory on the map" (Emmerson, 2001), mainly wrote about electrical communication systems. He studied coding and the effects of interference or noise, and his results suggest using more energy, for example, shouting louder, and exploiting redundancy which both reduce the probability of error in a noisy situation. Deliberately increasing redundancy in a sign can mean adding new features; a simple example is where more than one copy of a sign is deployed. Alternatively reducing the number of possible signs reduces the possibility of confusion, but for either technique, redundancy in one set of signs leaves less room for others.

Shannon (1948), like Hartley (1928) before him, acknowledged there was a semantic or psychological element in sign use but ignored it. Others, more interested in language, sought semantic functions. Karl Bühler (1990), for instance, reckoned in addition to being about something, signs indicate something about the sign-maker and also the attitude of sign-maker towards the sign-reader. Paul Watzlawick supposed signs incorporated "two orders of information" called the content and the relationship (Watzlawick and Beavin, 1967); he also stressed the importance of sequences of signs (Watzlawick et al., 1967, p.59). F. Schulz von Thun produced a hybrid model and also analysed the sign-reader's tasks and suggested, for example the sign-reader might ask, "Is the representation adequate, relevant or true?", "What is the sign-maker revealing about themselves?" and so on (von Thun, 1981).

What follows is a summary of the functions of signs derived from the work of these authors organised around the six categories recognised by Jakobson (1981) who most notably introduced a poetic function.

Referentials

The referential function reveals what a sign is about. One view is it relates the sign to something in the world. This view has been heavily criticised (Putnam, 1988), besides on encountering a sign the question is not "What does the sign represent?" but "What should I do?". One difficulty with a representational relation arises from the use of signs in fiction. The map of the fictional island Balnibarbi in Gulliver's Travels establishes a territory referred to in the text but does not exist elsewhere (Swift, 2001, p.157). Similarly, "Somerset county council erected . . . road signs . . . proclaiming 'Welcome to Somerset'.". These signs define what Somerset is to someone encountering a sign, unfortunately legal documents implied "the signs were a lie, since the county's border is 15 miles to the north" (Booker, 2004).

What Somerset is, as with Balnibarbi, is defined by the texts or signs you choose to use; the signs construct their objects.

C.S. Peirce, writing about a sign, concluded "we have, therefore, simply to determine what habits it produces, for what a thing means is simply what habits it involves", and he continued, "the identity of a habit depends on how it might lead us to act" (Peirce, 1878). Foucault effectively adopts Peirce's view when he describes a "referential", as a summary of habits in the form of "laws of possibilities, rules of existence for the objects that are named, designated, or described within it, and for the relations that are affirmed or denied within it" (Foucault, 1994, p.91). Discourses then become "practices that systematically form the objects of which they speak" (Foucault, 1994, p.49).

Money has often been used as an analogy in explaining language (Saussure, 1959, p.79; Parsons, 1963; Gray, 1996), and trade is a practice in which coins and goods are exchanged, where what matters is not what a coin refers to but that monetary exchanges are habitual; that is, money gets its significance from its use.

Time is also used in a variety of activities, for example, determining how long it takes to do a job hence how much it will cost, navigating in conjunction with the positions of the stars, regulating religious ceremonies or synchronising activities. Talk of time is, though, instrumental in these activities, for instance, if the train company sticks to the timetable, and I use my watch to arrive on time, I will catch the train. As long as all our clocks behave in a similar way, and we become proficient in reading them, then it does not matter what they refer to; clocks are signs that constitute time (Read, 2002; Callender, 2010).

The referential function of a sign then identifies the sign's use and constructs objects. But this does not explain how the sign catalyses a social practice. Richard Rorty provided a picture, which did not rely on the notion of representation, that usefully shows a relationship between an encounter with a sign and subsequent actions, the elements of practice. First he presented the self as a web of interconnected beliefs. The beliefs Rorty refers to are Peirce's "habits of action" that enable an observer to predict someone else's behaviour. All aspects of mental state, including emotions, moods and attitudes as well as what are commonly considered as beliefs, influence such predictions, so Rorty subtly shifts the use of the word 'beliefs'; his beliefs are intermodulated by other components of bodily and mental state so are partly product of moods and emotions (Rorty, 1991a). He set aside perception and assumed relations between the world and the web of beliefs are causal relations so a physical sign, when encountered, caused a new belief to 'pop up' creating a tension with other beliefs in the web. These tensions cause the web to reweave itself to reduce the strains. The degree of reaction, resistance and reshaping depends on the existing network of beliefs and the tensions within it (Rorty, 1991b).

The web of belief can also stimulate bodily movements via the muscles and the resulting actions "by shoving items in the environment around, produce new beliefs to be woven in, which in turn produce new actions". Some shoving will create signs which are therefore man-made, in other words, causally dependent on human beliefs, but signs can be produced by other processes. For Rorty the representative man-made object is a text; other objects he called "lumps", and the difference is "we know how to form and defend hypotheses about the author's intentions in the one case but not the other" (Rorty, 1991c).

With this picture the referential function defines the place of a sign in a sign game, but that place and hence the function will depend on the state of sign-reader's web of beliefs which will be altered by the encounter so a repeated encounter with a sign or encounter with a copy of a sign will generate a new function; and different selves with different histories and hence different webs of belief will experience referential functions that situate the sign in different places in the game or even in different games.

Expressive

The 'expressive', or 'emotive', function of a sign constructs an impression of the identity, state and attitude of the sender, which might be, for instance, ironic, humorous, serious or hyperbolic. Ignoring such expressive features in an analysis, Jakobson insists, "arbitrarily reduces the informational capacity of messages".

Examples of signs where the expressive function dominates are "burning tyres" (Lichfield, 2008) expressing anger in difficult times, and garbage in the street as a "statement of alienation" (Guest, 1991). Size and colour use can also be manifestations of the strength of feeling towards what the sign is about.

In Mesopotamia, during the Bronze Age, processed food was stored in jars sealed with clay and traded. A pattern embossed on the seal furnished evidence of the provenance of the goods and seals differentiated the products of different producers (Wengrow, 2008)—an expressive function. Thus the clay seals were a precursor of branding on packaging and the wax seal once used to authenticate documents (Anonymous, 2004).

Some objects have practical use yet simultaneously act as strongly expressive signs, for example, "since consumers cannot avoid wearing clothes, they are unable to prevent others from 'reading' meanings into the clothes they wear" (Campbell, 1997, p.349) and "Odour is . . . above all a statement of who one is" (Synnott, 1991). This latter example illustrates the possibility that the sign-reader can be the same person as the sign-writer and consequently expressive reflexivity can affect self-identity.

Conative

In explaining the conative function of the sign, Bühler draws an analogy with 'sex appeal'. An apt comparison since sexual appeals made in advertising are "attention getting, arousing, affect inducing, and memo-rable" (Reichert et al., 2001). The conative function also sets the modality of the sign, for instance, is the sign requesting, advising, instructing, urg-ing or commanding. Overall the conative function frames the sign-reader's attitude towards the sign, and thereby constructs something about the rela-tionship between the sign-writer and the sign-reader.

Many published analyses are limited to situations with one sender, who issues signs, for one receiver connected by a communications medium. The notion of appeal has special relevance where there is a wider audience and the sign is not intended for everyone. For instance, a branded package or label will commonly gain the attention of specific groups; an arrow direct-ing people at an airport might specifically address ticket holders heading for a flight with the label 'Departures' (Fuller, 2002); and traffic lights are pointed towards only those who are expected to respond.

Any kind of note, letter or e-mail will be directed to individuals and all these technologies will need some device for identifying the intended recipient that the recipients recognise. This could be done by exploiting aspects their self-image possibly just a name. Techniques for identifying and addressing individuals and groups through signs are therefore an inte-gral part of signs systems.

Phatic

Bronislaw Malinowski (1927) introduced the phrase "phatic commu-nion" for "speech in which ties of union are created by a mere exchange of words" and in which each utterance serves "the direct aim of binding hearer to speaker by a tie of some social sentiment or other". The tasks of signs exhibiting a phatic function are thus to create or maintain social bonds that in turn constitute institutions. Malinowski (1927) gave an example of the "binding tissue of words which unites the crew of a ship in bad weather" which implies first that a single utterance is not enough to generate secure institutional ties and second that the phatic function is interwoven with other sign functions in the exchanges that coordinate actions to sail the ship. Thus phatic functions marshal signs into networks and achieve their social objectives by exploiting the other sign functions in the resulting complexes.

Roman Jakobson (1981), following Malinowski, gave as an example of phatic elements the apparently petty utterances that prolong spoken com-munication but which inevitably establish a connection between preceding and following signs. Jakobson also included, as examples of signs with a phatic function, signs that establish and discontinue communication as well as the interjections that offer assurances that interlocutors have grasped the whole of a complex sign spread over time and space. Thus the material form of phatic communication binds together the parts of a complex sign and the effects of the complex can reinforce institutional relationships. Equally, by not binding, the phatic function can maintain a separation between complex signs and institutions.

An example of a sign that provides a phatic function and establishes the binding between other signs by simply filling in time or space and maintains the attention of the addressee is the use of music while a telephone caller is on hold. Signs can be segmented with a phatic component connect the parts. For example, the front page of a Sunday newspaper announced, "FREE INSIDE DR WHO AUDIOBOOK . . .". Inside were details of the offer followed by an asterisk which referred to a footnote. The footnote then referred the reader to the Monday edition of the newspaper for the conditions applying to the offer (ASA, 2010).

Bindings provide the cohesion between signs that constitute the moves in a sign game. An addressed and sealed envelope containing a letter firmly binds the letter to the address. But the address in its turn binds the envelope to a name on a street sign and to a numeral on a house. Bindings can therefore provide identification, for example, the law requires owners to ensure dogs in public places wear a collar carrying the owner's name and address (Gummer et al., 1992). Once labelled or named (Wittgenstein, 1992, §15) a symbolic binding can be made to the labelled object, for example, a text on a ticket for an event provides a symbolic binding to a seat at the named venue which has labelled seats and rows, and a clock.

Juxtaposition is a form of binding seen in price lists and tables such as the array of place names, typographical symbols, text and times that form a timetable (Esbester, 2009). A map too can be thought of as a collection of selected signs bound to specific positions on a substrate. People arranged in a queue bind themselves through their relative position to indicate their order of arrival and who is to be served next. Bodies are the tokens but since the signifier is arbitrary, bodies could be replaced by other signs. Copies of signs, or signs with common characteristics, bind to one another. A soldier's uniform for instance exhibits a phatic function which binds one soldier to others to create an outward sign of an army.

Because it binds signs in a complex together, the phatic function opens up the possibility of collaborative production of signs. For example, a passport constructs an identity from a collection of signs provided by a variety of institutions: a name, a photograph, a national symbol, a number from an issuing authority, stamps from places visited and so on. The phatic function of the passport forms a relationship between signs which allows each institution to avoid theorising about the origins of the contributions of other institutions and to treat any contribution as a mere attribution.

Pockets of money are also part of a collaboratively constructed sign. In a shop those providing the goods gain credit for their actions by pocketing cash from the buyer. Thus technologically a pocket of cash provides a memory of an individual's share of money as a heap of coins bound together and to an individual by being in a pocket (Kocherlakota, 1998). By adding and removing coins, the pocket effectively does the tallying. The same sort of thing can be done with a bank account, which is a binding between an identifier for the account holder and a promise of a sum of money. Given a description of the transaction, the bank performs the arithmetic but also invades the account holders' privacy (Andolfatto, 2009).

Phatic functions bind together signs constructed by players of an unfolding sign game to form a coherent discourse. Such discourses can create social bonds by, for example, instilling the feelings of stability, familiarity and affinity that constitute institutions such as bureaucracies, money systems, families and nations.

Meta-lingual

With its reliance on relationships between terms the meta-lingual function is a special kind of phatic function that helps translate features of a sign into other signs. Usually it relates the terms from one sign-using institution to terms from another. Examples include a key on a map relating symbols to a textual description or a caption on an artwork in a gallery. Jakobson points out the meta-lingual function plays a vital role in learning about a sign system.

Poetic

The poetic function relates a sign to itself and promotes "the palpability of signs" (Jakobson, 1981). One author offers illumination by placing the word 'aesthetic' alongside the term poetic (Waugh, 1980). Crucially poetics does not add "rhetorical adornment" (Jakobson, 1981); it pervades the whole sign. Since the other five functions are implicated in the sign, all are affected by poetics. An example is a "newspaper advertisement that employed a heavy black border to demarcate it from its neighbours" that consumers thought 'dead-looking', and were led to believe the advertised product was "impure" (Gardner and Levy, 1955). In this case, the poetic function was to do with the way the border was presented; the *use* of a border was part of the phatic function.

The choices available when constructing a sign provide the space for the poetic function to operate. Arranging and selecting components of the sign to form a pattern or rhythm or harmony are examples of aesthetic devices. The availability of unused channel such as odour, colour or music also gives scope for the poetic function to operate, for instance, by releasing the smell of hot bread in a supermarket (Mack, 2010).

One function of a sign is to draw attention to itself and is a function that might be subsumed into poetics.

CONCLUSIONS

Where we are fluent, the reaction to every sign becomes a reflex, and no explanation nor recourse to the vocabulary of 'information' is required; we are part of the institution, and all that is needed is volubility and faith in the sign game. Those with such a faith will be reluctant or unable to question the rituals of the game or seek alternative material forms even though within our institutions we can overcome physical limitations imposed by our signs by creating analogues with different material properties.

Inside a sign game, the referential function locates the sign within the game, the expressive and conative functions are acknowledgements of the possibility of interference between games and redundancy provides some protection from such hindrances. The meta-lingual function signals a recognition that there will be apprentices and infrequent players and the phatic function helps us to play sign games and build institutions and complex signs that span institutional boundaries. The poetic function provides an acknowledgement that sign making is itself a sign game.

The word 'information' enters when we try to stand outside of a sign game either because we wish to explain the operation of an institution or because we need to describe the connection between an institution we are a part of and another institution where we have little or no fluency. Information is therefore instrumental and attributed to signs which are produced in one institution but find a place in the sign games of another. Hence the term 'information' is employed within institutions devoted to sign production, such as psephology, sign transformation, such as computing or telecommunications and sign observation, such as organisational science, institutions that analyse or provide infrastructures for other institutions.

What makes a sign informative is that it has a place in someone's sign game. Thus an informative sign is one in which the referential function dominates; however, as a sign slides from one institution to another, what was its expressive, conative, phatic, meta-lingual or even poetic function can, in a new institution, become referential. For example, a referential function might be derived from an expressive function by psychologists interested in sign-makers or from a phatic function by telecommunications engineers interested in connections.

But once passed to a relevant institution, the informative signs inspire action, the signifieds drain away, and the signs become inseparable from reality. Or put another way, everything becomes a potential contributor to the sign game.

BIBLIOGRAPHY

Andolfatto, D. (2009) 'What Is Money? How Is It Created and Destroyed?', http://www.sfu.ca/%7Edandolfa/what%20is%20money.pdf (Accessed 15 October 2010).

Anonymous (1844) 'Foreign News', *Examiner*, London, no. 1891, 27 April, p.264.

Anonymous (1846) 'Information and Knowledge not Identical', *Examiner*, London, no. 2026, 28 November, p.753.

Anonymous (1847) 'Glances at Men and Books—No. II', *The Morning Post*, London, no. 22823, 27 January, p.5.

Anon. (2004) 'Seals', National Archives, http://www.nationalarchives.gov.uk/catalogue/RdLeaflet.asp?sLeafletID=225 (Accessed 25 July 2010).

ASA (2010) *Advertising Standards Authority Adjudication on Telegraph Media Group Ltd*, ref 124604, 21 July.

Basu, D. (1975) 'Statistical Information and Likelihood', *Sankhyā: The Indian Journal of Statistics*, Series A, vol. 37, no. 1, pp.1–71.

Booker, C. (2004) 'A Borderline Case', *Sunday Telegraph*, 22 August, p.14.

Brown, J.S. and Duguid, P. (2002) *The Social Life of Information*, Boston, Harvard Business School Press.

Bühler, K. (1990) *Theory of Language: The Representational Function of Language*, translated from German by D.F. Goodwin, Amsterdam, John Benjamins.

Callender, C. (2010) 'Is Time an ILLUSION?', *Scientific American*, vol. 302, no. 6, pp.58–65.

Campbell, C. (1997) 'When the Meaning Is Not a Message: A Critique of the consumption as Communication Thesis', in Nava, M., Blake, A., MacRury, I. and Richards, B. (eds.), *Buy This Book: Studies in Advertising and Consumption*, London, Routledge, pp.340–351.

de Saussure, F. (1959) *Course in General Linguistics,* 3rd ed., edited by C. Bally and A. Reidlinger, translated from French by W. Baskin, New York, Philosophical Library.

Edison, T.A. (1878) 'The Phonograph and Its Future', *The North American Review*, vol. 126, no. 262, pp.527–536.

Emmerson, A. (2001) 'Claude Shannon', *The Guardian*, 8 March, p.28.

Engelberg, J. and Boyarsky, L.L. (1979) 'The Noncybernetic Nature of Ecosystems', *American Naturalist*, vol. 114, no. 3, pp. 317–324.

Esbester, M. (2009) 'Designing Time: The Design and Use of Nineteenth-Century Transport Timetables', *Journal of Design History,* vol. 22, no. 2, pp.91–113.

Fisher, R.A. (1922) 'On the Mathematical Foundations of Theoretical Statistics', *Philosophical Transactions of the Royal Society of London,* Series A, vol. 222, pp.309–368.

Foucault, M. (1994) *Archaeology of Knowledge*, London, Routledge.

Fuller, G. (2002) 'The Arrow—Directional Semiotics: Wayfinding in Transit', *Social Semiotics*, vol. 12. no. 3, pp.231–244.

Gardner, B.B. and Levy, S.J. (1955) 'The Product and the Brand', *Harvard Business Review*, vol. 33, no. 2, pp.33–39.

Gray, R.T. (1996) 'Buying into Signs: Money and Semiosis in Eighteenth-Century German Language Theory', *The German Quarterly*, vol. 69, no. 1, pp.1–14.

Guest, I. (1991) 'Trashing New York's Garbage Cops', *The Guardian*, 28 June, p.32.

Gummer, J.S., Stewart, A. and Hunt, D. (1992) *Control of Dogs Order 1992*, Statutory Instrument 1992 no. 901, 19 March.

Hartley, R.V.L. (1928) 'Transmission of Information', *Bell System Technical Journal*, vol. 7, no. 3, pp.535–563.

Jakobson, R. (1981) 'Linguistics and Poetics', in Rudy, S. (ed.) *Roman Jakobson Selected Writings*, vol. 3, The Hague, Morton, pp.18–51.

Kocherlakota, N.R. (1998) 'Money Is Memory', *Journal of Economic Theory*, vol. 81, no. 2, pp.232–251.

Krippendorf, K. (1993) 'Major Metaphors of Communication and Some Constructivist Reflections on their Use', *Cybernetics and Human Knowing*, vol. 2, no. 1, pp.3–25.

Kruk, S. (2010) 'Profit Rather Than Politics: The Production of Lenin Monuments in Soviet Latvia', *Social Semiotics*, vol. 20, no. 3, pp.247–276.

Lichfield, J. (2008) 'High Spirits in Cognac', *The Independent*, 2 February, p.30.

Maandi, P. (2009) 'The Silent Articulation of Private Land Rights in Soviet Estonia: A Geographical Perspective', *Geoforum,* vol. 40, no. 3, pp.454–464.

Mack, A. (2010) 'Speaking of Tomatoes: Supermarkets, the Senses, and Sexual Fantasy in Modern America' *Journal of Social History*; vol. 43, no. 4, pp.815–842.

Malinowski, B.W. (1927) 'The Problem of Meaning in Primitive Languages', in Ogden, C. and Richards, I. (eds.), *The Meaning of Meaning*, London, Kegan Paul, pp.296–336.

Parsons, T. (1963) 'On the Concept of Influence', *The Public Opinion Quarterly*, vol. 27, no. 1, pp.37–62.

Peirce, C.S. (1878) 'Illustrations of the Logic of Science', *The Popular Science Monthly*, vol. 12, pp.286–302.

Putnam, H. (1988) *Representation and Reality*, Cambridge, Massachusetts, MIT Press.

Read, R. (2002) 'Is 'What Is Time?' A Good Question to Ask?', *Philosophy*, vol. 77, no. 300, pp.193–209.

Reichert, T., Heckler, S.E. and Jackson, S. (2001) 'The Effects of Sexual Social Marketing Appeals on Cognitive Processing and Persuasion', *Journal of Advertising*, vol. 30, no. 1, pp.13–27.

Rorty, R. (1991a) 'Inquiry as Recontextualization', in Rorty, R. *Objectivity, Relativism and Truth*, Cambridge, Cambridge University Press.

Rorty, R. (1991b) 'Non-Reductive Physicalism', in Rorty, R. *Objectivity, Relativism and Truth*, Cambridge, Cambridge University Press.

Rorty, R. (1991c) 'Text and Lumps', in Rorty, R. *Objectivity, Relativism and Truth*, Cambridge, Cambridge University Press.

Royal and Ancient (2010) Definition of a Flagstick from http://www.randa.org/en/Equipment/Equipment%20Rules.aspx#equipment (Accessed 29 July 2010).

Scroggie, J. (2008) 'Hands That Speak Volumes', *The Daily Telegraph*, 16 October, p.25.

Shannon, C.E. (1948) 'A Mathematical Theory of Information', *Bell Systems Technical Journal*, vol. 27, no. 3, pp.379–423 and pp.623–656.

Swift, J. (2001) *Gulliver's Travels*, London, Penguin.

Synnott, A. (1991) 'A Sociology of Smell', *Canadian Review of Sociology*, vol. 28, no. 4, pp.437–459.

von Foerster, H. (1970). 'Thoughts and Notes on Cognition', in Garvin, P. (ed.), *Cognition: A Multiple View*, New York, Spartan Books, pp.25–48.

von Schiller, C.F. (2005) 'William Tell', in *Schiller Vol 3*, translated from German by R.D. Macdonald, London, Oberon, pp.134–245.

von Thun, F.S. (1981) *Miteinander reden: Störungen und Klärungen. Psychologie der zwischenmenschlichen Kommunikation*, Reinbek, Rowohlt.

Watzlawick P. and Beavin J. (1967) 'Some Formal Aspects of Communication', *American Behavioral Scientist*, vol. 10, no. 8, pp.4–8.

Watzlawick, P., Beavin, J. and Jackson, D.D. (1967) *Pragmatics of Human Communication. A Study of Interactional Patterns, Pathologies, and Paradoxes*, New York, Norton.

Waugh, L.R. (1980) 'The Poetic Function in the Theory of Roman Jakobson', *Poetics Today*, vol. 2, no. 1a, pp.57–82.

Wengrow, D. (2008) Prehistories of Commodity Branding', *Current Anthropology*, vol. 49, no. 1, pp.7–34.

Wittgenstein, L. (1992) *Philosophical Investigations*, translated from German by G.E.M. Anscombe, Oxford, Blackwell.

6 Fundamentals of Information
Purposeful Activity, Meaning and Conceptualisation

Sue Holwell

ACTION AND APPRECIATION

> It is much easier to talk about information than it is to say what it is you are talking about. . . . A surprising number of books, and this includes textbooks, have the word information in their title without bothering to include it in their index. It has come to be an all-purpose word, one with suggestive power to fulfil a variety of descriptive tasks. (Dretske, 1981, p. ix)

This contribution is adapted from the book *Information, Systems and Information Systems: Making Sense of the Field* (Checkland and Holwell, 1998), and the reader is referred to that book for a comprehensive and richer account of the ideas outlined here.

It is satisfying to contribute to a book that addresses the fundamental concept of information from several disciplinary perspectives for a trans-disciplinary audience. In such a volume, it is helpful if an author is clear about the parameters they are working with. To that end: this is a contribution from the Information Systems (IS) field, a relatively new field that has emerged out of the experiences of computer systems being deployed in organisations. Information Systems has two clear characteristics: it exhibits some conceptual confusion, and there are two very distinct strands of thought in its literature.

We can take its core concern is taken to be the orderly provision of data and information in (and between) organisations and/or their members using information technology (IT), the purpose of which is to influence action. This most basic expression is broad enough to include the provision of information inter-organisationally (between separate organisations) and to loose networks of people who are not part of some formal organisation (a virtual organisation). Even if we take this most basic starting point then some concepts are crucial to it.

These are the fundamental concepts: information, information system, organisation, providing support, information technology. And, given how quickly the technology is changing, then, how we think about them has to take account of change.

The statement that the IS field is conceptually confused is argued in more detail elsewhere (Checkland and Holwell, 1998; Holwell, 1997) and for now the following broad statements paint the picture. There is confusion about many things. The concepts and body of knowledge are confused, divergent and not agreed, illustrated by having multiple versions of its history and development (such as many versions of its multi-disciplinary origins); and there are confusing and contradictory research findings. Within the IS literature, there are two very different strands of thinking, each with quite different premises and concepts, one of which is dominant.

Many authors have discussed the inadequacy of the dominant strand of IS thinking, which takes as its foundation an objective reality, containing functional, goal-seeking organisations that require support for task-related decision-making using value-free data. However, there remains an absence of a coherent theoretical and conceptual framework and language (Holwell, 1997).

This is a contribution towards rectifying this absence by exploring the inter-relationships between the fundamental concepts of: people acting purposefully, the 'information' that they use, the information systems that handle 'information' and the mechanisms that deliver information systems within a single coherent framework.

I will draw extensively upon the concept of appreciative systems outlined by Geoffrey Vickers (1965; 1968; 1970; 1983; 1984). Vickers describes the continuous process by which humans perceive, make judgements and act accordingly, during their participation in human affairs. His conceptualisation was the outcome of reflecting on forty years' experience in public life.

He describes the "actual social process which characterises human communication and action" (Checkland and Casar, 1986, p.4) through the concept of 'appreciation' and its operation through an 'appreciative system'. The key themes in Vickers' works that set out 'appreciation' are

- the concept of day-to-day experienced life as a flux of interacting events and ideas
- a separation of judgements about what is the case (reality judgements) and judgements about what is good or bad (value judgements)
- relationship maintaining as a richer concept of human action than the popular notion of goal-seeking
- a concept of action judgements stemming from reality and value judgements
- the notion that the cycle of judgements and actions are organised as a system (Checkland and Casar, 1986).

The starting point for his model is the flux of interacting events and ideas unfolding through time:

Thus human history is a two-stranded rope; the history of events and the history of ideas developed in intimate relation with each other yet each according to its own logic and its own time scale; and each conditions both its own future and the future of the other. (Vickers, 1965, p.15)

The flux of events and ideas is perceived through the 'appreciative setting' or 'net' which acts as a kind of cognitive filter through which reality is perceived and interpreted (Holwell, 1989):

experience . . . develops in each of us readinesses to notice particular aspects of our situation, to discriminate them in particular ways and to measure them against particular standards of comparison. . . . [T]hese readinesses in turn help to further organise experience. (Vickers, 1970, p.102)

Vickers argued that the world as we appreciate it is "carved out by our interests, structured by our expectations and evaluated by our standards of judgement" (1970, p.98), which as Peter Checkland later observed implies that "the readinesses to see and value things in one way rather than another are organised in an appreciative system which creates, individually and socially, our appreciated world" (Checkland, 1981, p.263). The standards that Vickers refers to are standards of fact and value, the source of which is *the previous history of the system itself.* These standards may be modified by the act of using them.

Vickers argued that the judgements we make about the world are of three kinds—reality judgements, which are "judgements of fact about the 'state of the system'" (Vickers, 1968, p.138); value judgements, which are "judgements of the significance of these facts" (ibid., p.139); and instrumental, or action judgements. He observed that

The relation between judgements of fact and of value is close and mutual; for facts are relevant only in relation to some judgement of value and judgements of value are operative only in relation to some configuration of fact. (Vickers, 1965, p.40)

The system is dynamic; its content (standards and appreciative acts and appreciative setting) changes over time, but its overall form remains. Our previous experience creates in us standards and norms and concepts of what are good and bad. These standards, norms and values lead to readinesses to notice only certain aspects of our situations; they determine what facts are relevant (and noticed). As Checkland (1985, p.761–762) observes:

'appreciation' [is] a mental, evaluative act in which conflicting norms and values determine what 'facts' are relevant, whilst 'facts' perceived or envisaged demand attention because they are seen to be relevant to

> particular norms and values. . . . These 'facts' are evaluated against the standards, which lead to actions with respect to relationship managing and also modify our standards

Vickers incorporates the concept of relationship maintaining having rejected both the goal-seeking model of organisations and the steering metaphor from cybernetics:

> the goal-seeking paradigm is inadequate. Regulatory activity, in government, management or private life consists in attaining or maintaining desired relationships through time or in changing and eluding undesired ones. (Vickers quoted in Checkland and Casar, 1986, p.16)

Thus actions are selected through the operation of the appreciative system in terms of managing relationships. Within the appreciative systems model, the actions taken are understood in terms of relationship maintaining rather than as a means to achieve goals (Checkland and Casar, 1986).

Sperber and Wilson (1986) provide an explanation of the cognitive processing that is at the centre of the appreciative process. Their argument is that context is a set of premises: a psychological construct used in interpreting an utterance (or an appreciative setting in interpreting events and ideas), which includes the physical environment, preceding events and ideas, future expectations, hypotheses, beliefs, memories and cultural assumptions. Experience adds to the potential range of contexts. Differences in cognitive abilities (perceptual, inferential, mastery of concepts and memories) mean that each person has a different cognitive environment and set of contexts, and therefore a different mental representation of the world.

The cognitive environment (i.e. the set of readinesses to notice some things and not to notice others) consists of manifest 'facts' that are capable of being represented mentally, accepted as being true or probably true, of which you are either aware or capable of becoming aware.

The world is interpreted through this stock of assumptions of fact. These are structured sets of concepts and include both those that express values and attitudes and also incomplete "assumption schemata" (Sperber and Wilson, 1986, p.167) that are completed on the basis of contextual information. General concepts such as 'chair' fall into the latter category. These factual assumptions have associated with them a degree of confidence, i.e. they are more or less true. Context information and synthesis of new and old information may confirm a schema, contradict it or even cause rejection of it.

And so, appreciation occurs by adding new assumptions, completing incomplete schemata and varying the associated degrees of confidence.

Processing is organised to obtain the greatest benefit for the minimum effort and so relevance, a multiplier effect from new information, is a determinant of whether to notice or not to notice something. Because new information requires effort, connections are made to old information, and additional information is then derived or inferred from premises based on both the old and new information. You notice what is more manifest and relevant, and that is what you choose to process.

A FRAMEWORK FOR INFORMATION SYSTEMS FUNDAMENTALS

These key ideas distilled from Vickers' work, supported by the argument of Sperber and Wilson, form the scaffolding for a coherent framework for thinking about IS fundamentals but require some re-statement for that purpose.

The obvious place to begin is to consider the process at a personal or individual level. As human beings we are conscious of an external world and of ourselves and others as part of that world.

We can re-express Vickers' appreciative system model to give a basic model of the *human* agent acting in the world. People perceive selected parts of the world, attribute some meanings to what they perceive, make judgements about their perceptions, on the basis of these judgements form intentions to take actions, and then act. The consequential change to the perceived world (the flux of events and ideas) from both judgements and actions, however slight, means that the process begins again, becoming a cycle. The appreciative system is always a product of the previous history of the system itself and its interactions with its environment.

We always selectively perceive parts of the flux, filtered as a result of our interests and previous history—Vickers describes readinesses to notice some things and not notice other things created by previous judgements. Consider, for example, an area of land on a picturesque part of the Scottish coast. This might be perceived very differently by a golfer and a botanist. Each of these have a framework (an appreciative setting or cognitive filter) derived from their interests and experience which structures their perceptions.

Attributing meaning and making judgements of fact and value to what is perceived, implies the existence of standards or criteria against which assessment can be made. The standards need not be given from outside—they are generated by the previous history of the system itself and its interactions with its environment. The standards will themselves change over time as new experience accumulates.

As soon as we make a judgement, such as considering some part of the Scottish coast as 'botanically important', succeeding perceptions and attributions of meaning will be different from those made in the absence of that judgement. Remember that the judgements may concern either what is perceived or the standards used to judge what is perceived. So we may begin to pay attention to something we have previously not noticed, or we may judge something differently to which we have previously paid attention.

The personal level model is of an individual selectively perceiving his or her world, judging it, and taking intentional action in the light of those perceptions and judgements. Importantly, the individual who does not conform to the commonly shared perceptions, meaning attributions and judgements (despite social or political pressure to do so) does not nullify this model.

However, the most basic notion of information support suggests that an isolated individual acting in the world is of much less interest than the broader social process. Each person has the potential to perceive and interpret the world in an entirely unique way, but humans are social creatures with an extensive language; and our perceptions, interpretations and judgements about the world will be shaped by our exchanges with others.

These exchanges are enacted via the non-stop discussion, dialogue and debate through which we try to affect each others perceptions, judgements, intentions and actions (appreciative system in Vickers' language; cognitive environment for Sperber and Wilson). From this we can assume that much of the previously individual cognitive activity will occur in discourse (all communications where the purpose is to affect the thinking and actions of at least one other). Thus, Robinson Crusoe and Man Friday could enact their own personal models until they met, but having met, they must engage in discourse, i.e. communication.

So, in the social process leading to purposeful or intentional action model, appreciative settings lead to particular aspects of situations, as well as 'situations' themselves, being noticed and judged in particular ways using standards built up from past experience. Accommodations which lead to action being taken may be reached out of the resulting discourse. Importantly, both the appreciative settings and the standards by which judgements are made may be changed by the appreciation, judgement or action. They inevitably change through time as our personal and social history develop.

The notion of appreciative settings described in both the individual and social processes is not limited to individuals. Personal settings are unique, but they often overlap with those of people with whom we are connected or who have had similar experiences. In practice, appreciative settings may be attributed to a group of people, for instance, to members of a team, or department, or organisation. However, in doing this we must remember that there will *never* be complete correspondence between individual and attributed group settings.

So far I have taken appreciation as the conceptual foundation, and developed accounts of personal and social level processes leading to purposeful action being taken. Now, using the same framework, we can think about information systems, taking a step closer to 'information'—the central focus of this volume.

This time we start with people taking purposeful action, as a result of having engaged in the social processes. Information systems usually serve or support this social process. Sometimes these are formal, designed systems (as you might find in a corporation) and other times informal and evolutionary (as you might find in a family).

The third necessary element is to recognise that all information systems are embodied in some technology, often computer based, although not necessarily. So, the information system is different to the technology and each must be thought about specifically. Three necessary and inter-connected elements manifest, influence and affect each other: the social process, information systems that support it and the technology that makes the IS. Thus the invention of new technologies for implementing information systems makes new kinds of IS feasible, which, in turn, may make new ideas and new kinds of purposeful activity possible or feasible.

Frank Land's pragmatically derived model of an information system is quite compatible with the argument above. It includes a person who perceives the world through a cognitive filter which will "select, amplify, reject, attenuate or distort" messages (Land, 1985, p.212). Action to be taken is determined by the association of the messages received (from whatever source—a formal IS, informal sources or from the world itself) with knowledge stored in a person's memory. Land's conclusion is that "an information system is a social system which has embedded in it information technology . . . it is not possible to design a robust, effective information system incorporating significant amounts of the technology without treating it as a social system" (ibid., p.215).

Land's argument includes the point that the meanings derived from the association of messages and a person's memory create information and knowledge which will lead to accommodations being made, intentions being formed and purposeful action undertaken. Both the thinking and the action change the perceived world and may change the cognitive filter for our perceptions. Such a process is cyclic and never-ending.

A further relevant perspective from the broad IS literature is that of Daft and Weick (1984), who argue that organisations ought to be taken to be 'interpretation systems' in which members scan their world, collect data about it (or rather capta in the terms later discussed in this chapter) which is then interpreted (given meaning) so that action can be taken.

INFORMATION IN SUPPORT OF ACTION

If there was agreement about the core concepts of IS, in particular data and information, then this volume would not be either necessary or interesting. However, that is not the case as Liebenau and Backhouse (1990) illustrated twenty years ago when they listed ten very different definitions of 'information'.

So far in this chapter, I have set out an idea of the inherent social process being enacted, and by implication, a notion of 'organization' that encompasses multiple interpretations and subversive members and also made clear the relationships between people taking purposeful action, information systems supporting them and the technology that enables the information system. We can now explore the concept of 'information'. If we take the core concern of IS as being the orderly provision of 'information', then we can now say that 'information' is something needed in support of the purposeful action that goes on in organisations. The argument is that if organisational action is to be well-informed, better than playing hunches, then information is needed to support the action-taking.

Just as there were subtleties to consider in thinking about 'organization', any concept of 'information' also has to handle some subtle characteristics. Anderton (1991) gives three interesting examples, one of which is as follows.

A traveller needs to fly abroad at short notice, but he can do so only if he is not infected with or carrying smallpox. He has a test in the afternoon of the intended day of travel. If the results are positive, the doctor will notify the check-in desk before 17:00. At 17:00 he confirms that no message has been received at the desk and so receives the information that he is free of smallpox. Yet no tangible event has occurred, and nothing has carried the information that he can travel.

Checkland and Holwell (1998) give another example. Details of several rock climbs on Salisbury Crags in Edinburgh's Holyrood Park have long been published, and climbers have been following them since the 1890s. Current climbing guides describe several climbs in detail but notes that because climbing on any cliff in the park is illegal, the route descriptions are reproduced for their historical interest. The message conveyed to an experienced rock climber is not what the note says. To them, the guidebook is saying there are some good climbs, enjoy them but be careful and have a good story ready! In other words what is conveyed is virtually the opposite of what the wording actually says.

What is needed is an account of 'data', 'information' and the relationship between them which makes sense of such examples. We cannot start by asking what do the words 'data' and 'information' mean? However we can explore both what distinctions are useful to make and the process through which we make use of the words ('data', 'information', 'knowledge') which denote the distinctions.

Holwell's (1989) concept of information as four linked elements, *data* plus *meaning* (interpretation) in a particular *context* at a particular *time,* separately identifies meaning as the basic inferences or deductions that may be drawn from data and the context as being the set of premises through which the meaning is interpreted at a particular time. A change in one component has potential consequential flow on effects to one or more of the others. This is an extension to Checkland's (1981) definition of information as data + meaning and Anderton's statement that: "meaning . . . comes from its *moment-to-moment interpretation* in terms of a rich, shared unspoken *background* of concerns and experiences. The meaning is not to be found in a formal representation of a supposed objective world" (Anderton, 1989, p.118).

Two points are relevant here: first, that meaning is dependent on context and second, that a person's appreciative setting is a necessary factor. In the work of the authors described above, these resulted in the redefinition of 'information' to include *context* at a particular *time*. So, meaning depends on an *agent's* appreciative setting which is both unique and shaped by the context in which the agent operates.

FROM DATA TO CAPTA

So far the notion of appreciation has been used to shape accounts of both a personal and social process and a conceptualisation of organisation. The provision of information support to people acting purposefully has been discussed. Now using the same set of notions, we turn to consideration of the core concept—'information'.

A reasonable starting point is that there are innumerable facts about the world (and that they can be stated neutrally). For instance, it is fact that the author of this chapter was born in Melbourne, and that she is a member of a golf club. Both of these facts are verifiable and, if queried, evidence could be produced to confirm or disprove them. There is an abundance (some would say an overabundance) of such facts. Some of these are agreed by all, some are disputed, some are accepted as meaningful by all and some are meaningful only to an individual or group because of very particular interests (appreciative settings, or cognitive environments).

The first distinction to make is between the great mass of facts available and the subset of them which we select for attention, those which we actually notice. We do not and cannot perceive everything possible about the world—we are selective. The word used for the mass of facts is 'data', from the Latin *dare*, meaning 'to give'. But there is no existing word for the selection of the available data that we actually notice, know or create. So for a kind of consistency, that data which we have decided is relevant and which we therefore know we want to collect is referred to as 'capta', from the Latin *capere*, meaning 'to take' (Checkland, 1982).

This distinction is the starting point. Data are available to us, and capta are the result of consciously selecting some data for attention or creating some new category—such as 'the number of golf club members living in Watford' or becoming aware of some items of data which we begin to pay attention to. This process of turning data into capta has become so familiar it is transparent—we do it but don't notice the process occurring.

Having selected, paid attention to or created some data, thereby turning it into capta, we *attribute meaning* to it. We relate it to other things, we put it in context (which may be cognitive, spatial or temporal), seeing it as a part of a larger whole (Holwell, 1989). The attribution of meaning in context converts capta into something different and so another word is needed: the everyday definition of the word *information* suggests that it is appropriate.

This individual and/or collective process, by which data is selected and converted into meaningful information, can lead to larger assemblies of related information for which another word is needed—here we can use the word *knowledge*. These structures of information are expected to be longer lasting. The following example comes from Checkland and Holwell (1998, p.90):

> [At] a particular point in time in a home furnishing company, managers might select as *capta*, from all their sales *data*, the figures concerning the sales of a new expensive kitchen chair, aggregated separately for each sales area over the last three months. In the context of introducing this new product, these capta would yield *information* concerning, for example, the readiness of people in different geographical areas, classified socio-economically, to buy a basic but expensive product. This would itself contribute to updating the company's larger-scale slower-moving *knowledge* of the home furnishing market.

So this schema (illustrated in Figure 6.1) describes four notions: data, capta, information and knowledge. It is marked by three distinctions created by

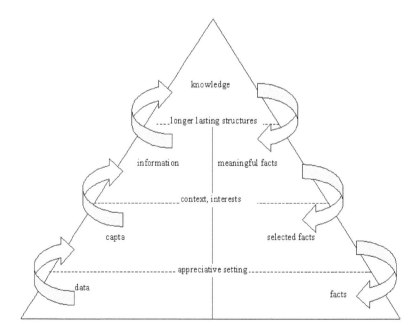

Figure 6.1 Data, capta, information and knowledge. Adapted from Checkland and Holwell, 1998, p. 90.

our actions of: *selecting* data, *attributing meaning* to this selected data, and *assembling* larger structures of meaningful data.

The most important feature of this schema is that the act of creating information is a *human* act. It is the human being alone who can attribute meaning to the data which has been selected for attention, in a context which may be shared by many people or may be unique to an individual. Clearly the *designer* of an information system which processes capta will have the aim of making the processed capta correspond to some obvious categories of information which will be meaningful to different people using the information system, but no designer can guarantee that their intended attributions of meaning will be recognised or accepted. So, capta selected from sales data will yield different information to different people: the salesman gets information about his bonus, the director gets information about the introduction of a new product, and the production manager get information about the increased number of process workers needed.

Using this schema we can make sense of the earlier example about the smallpox test where the absence of any message conveys information to the traveller, even though nothing has carried the information, powerfully illustrating the importance of context in getting information from data. The arrangement with the doctor establishes a context in which the absence of any message before 17:00 itself conveys meaningful information.

In the second example, in which the writer of the rock-climbing guide manages to convey a message which is virtually the opposite of what the words say, we have another example of the important part which *context* plays in creating information. Many people looking at the guide would accept at face value the statement that climbing is illegal. But a rock climber has an appreciative setting that incorporates attitudes and values shared by the rock-climbing fraternity and if caught and challenged would adopt an air of innocence. This is a paper-based example of the familiar everyday passing of information between members of a particular group by a tone of voice, hand gesture or wink.

Whilst the IS field has no sharp definitions of 'data', 'information' and 'knowledge' that are generally accepted (Liebenau and Backhouse, 1990), there is a collection of ideas that sits comfortably with the argument here. Commonly we find that 'data' refers to 'raw facts' or 'raw material', and virtually all definitions of 'information' use the word 'data' to describe the starting material out of which information is created via some process like 'interpret', 'transform', 'process', 'assemble', with words like 'meaning', 'value', 'useful', 'relevant' also being included.

They present a basic view that data is transformed into information when 'meaning' is attributed to it, but because they do not include the crucial element that meaning attribution is done by people, it cannot cover the possibility that different people may attribute different meanings to the same data, or, different meanings at different times. This is a major exclusion. However the biggest deficiency, in terms of this analysis, is that no distinction is made between the enormous mass of data which could be selected for processing and the small amount which actually gets selected. The process which turns data into capta is fundamental, not least because what information systems do is to *process capta*; therefore, a prior selection process to distinguish some capta from the mass of data is unavoidable.

BIBLIOGRAPHY

Anderton, R.H. (1989) 'From Policies and Plans to Conversations and Commitments', *Journal of Applied Systems Analysis*, vol. 16, pp.117–120.

Anderton, R.H. (1991) 'Information and Systems', *Journal of Applied Systems Analysis*, vol. 18, pp.57–60.

Checkland, P.B. (1981) *Systems Thinking, Systems Practice*, Chichester, John Wiley and Sons.

Checkland, P.B. (1982) 'An Organised Research Programme? In Information Systems?', Internal Discussion Paper No. IDP 1/82, Lancaster, Department of Systems and Information Management, Lancaster University.

Checkland, P.B. (1985) 'From Optimizing to Learning: A Development of Systems Thinking for the 1990s', *Journal of the Operational Research Society*, vol. 36, no. 9, pp.757–767.

Checkland, P.B. and Casar, A. (1986) 'Vickers' Concept of an Appreciative System: A Systemic Account', *Journal of Applied Systems Analysis*, vol. 13, pp.3–17.

Checkland, P.B. and Holwell, S.E. (1998) *Information, Systems and Information Systems: Making Sense of the Field*, Chichester, John Wiley and Sons.

Daft, R. and Weick, K. (1984) 'Towards a Model of Organizations as Interpretation Systems', *Academy of Management Review*, vol. 9, pp.284–295.

Dretske, F.I. (1981) *Knowledge and the Flow of Information*, Oxford, Blackwell.

Holwell, S.E. (1989) *Planning in Shell: Joint Learning through Action Research*, unpublished MSc, Lancaster University, Lancaster.

Holwell, S.E. (1997) *Soft Systems Methodology and Its Role in Information Systems*, unpublished PhD, Lancaster University, Lancaster.

Land, F.F. (1985) 'Is an Information Theory Enough?', *The Computer Journal*, vol. 28, no. 3, pp.211–216.

Liebenau, J. and Backhouse, J. (1990) *Understanding Information: An Introduction*. Basingstoke, MacMillan Education Ltd.

Sperber, D. and Wilson, D. (1986) *Relevance: Communication and Cognition*, Oxford, Blackwell.

Vickers, G. (1965) *The Art of Judgement: A Study of Policy Making*, London, Chapman and Hall.

Vickers, G. (1968) *Value Systems and Social Process*, London, Tavistock.

Vickers, G. (1970) *Freedom in a Rocking Boat: Changing Values in an Unstable Society*, London, Allen Lane.

Vickers, G. (1983) *Human Systems Are Different*, London, Harper and Row.

Vickers, G. (1984) *The Vickers Papers*, London, Harper and Row.

7 Using Information (and Exformation) to Inform Action

Paul Lefrere

INTRODUCTION

The ubiquity of the term 'information' (and its kin, information *society*, *explosion* and *overload*) means that at a day-to-day level we risk taking information for granted. What we need is a way to *problematise* the notion of information, to view with fresh eyes our ways of noticing, sharing and interpreting it. That is one of the challenges we face in this chapter. Another challenge is that we are only human; and so our cognitive abilities are very limited; we are inattentive and easily distracted; we are poor at noticing things that we do not expect to see; and we misinterpret coincidences as causal relationships (e.g. Chabris and Simons, 2010).

Like the proverbial African child, whom it 'took a whole village to raise', everyone and everything in our environment has an influence on how we think and what we think, both in general and in respect of 'information'. I am aware of—and indeed cannot fully escape—some of the influences I was subject to, as I was 'raised by', or exposed to, various 'villages' in my life (e.g. home, school, work, societal, academic disciplines). For example, I have a research background in Science, Engineering, Education, Psychology and Management and look often at journals in those areas, but I rarely read journals from Arts and Humanities, limiting myself to coffee-table books. Inevitably, my familiarity with quantitative approaches, coupled with my relative ignorance of professional concerns in the Arts, introduces biases into my views about how information is conceived in the Arts. Additionally, like everyone, I am subject to various general judgemental biases, part of human decision making, which have for decades been the subject of academic study (e.g. in the field of behavioural economics). Given the impact of biases and gaps, I devote part of this chapter to looking at how to reduce their effects, e.g. by sensitising ourselves to—then compensating for—any tendency we have to pay too much attention to some kinds of information (for example, expressed mathematically) and too little to other kinds.

THE VON NEUMANN ERA

I begin with the early days of formalised models of information and decision making based upon them (e.g. economic-utility models and the theory of games and rational decision making, as in von Neumann and Morgenstern, 1944). Not being an historian, my sense of the zeitgeist of that era is influenced by anecdotes from the 1940s, e.g. as recounted in the television series *The Ascent of Man* (Bronowski, 1973). They suggest to me that scientism (in the strong sense of belief in the universal applicability of science and mathematics and the lack of need for any other approach) was attractive to von Neumann and maybe other research pioneers. Their work was groundbreaking, so some arrogance (as in scientism) would be understandable, if unpalatable to people who found their work hard to understand. The latter group included many non-scientists at the time; a decade later, that lack of understanding was infamously characterised by CP Snow as the emergence of two cultures: science and arts.

The scientists, mathematicians and engineers of the time made major advances in machines and systems to transmit, receive and interpret data, and as part of that, to do some of the following to it: encode, decode, manipulate, codify. This yielded insights into ways to store and retrieve data securely and reliably and ways to select and analyse data that yield high value information. The 1940s examples of advances, influential today, include models of communication under noisy conditions (e.g. Shannon, 1948), identification of potentially loss-less ways to record information (the hologram: Gabor, 1948) and the Memex (Bush, 1945) with its imagined hyperlink-like mechanisms, useful for information retrieval, annotation, sharing and creating a collective memory.

Those remarkable achievements and others (including ones that some of us might regret, such as the atomic bomb), raised the status of scientists and meant that their pronouncements were often accepted without question even when they were on matters far from the area of expertise of the speaker. Gradually that deference to scientists declined, partly as it became apparent that scientific advances brought social dilemmas that needed a humanistic perspective as part of a systemic perspective (e.g. today we see that medical breakthroughs enable old people to live longer but have implications for pension schemes and that secure communications enable safe financial transactions but can be used by terrorists). Cross-disciplinary views on information might bring new insights into such dilemmas.

The various perspectives were familiar to Jacob Bronowski, as a polymath (biologist, chess contestant, literary editor, mathematician), and enabled him post-war to become a renowned radio and television presenter, where he expounded on science, ethics, philosophy and much else.

> science is also a source of power that walks close to government and that the state wants to harness. . . . It is not the business of science to

inherit the earth, but to inherit the moral imagination; because without that man and beliefs and science will perish together. (Bronowski, 1973, p.419)

Although a polymath, unlike von Neumann, he was not a genius.

COMMUNICATING AND USING INFORMATION

The mathematician John von Neumann shaped our views on information through fundamental contributions in cellular automata, computer science, continuous geometry, economics, ergodic theory, functional analysis, game theory, hydrodynamics, quantum mechanics, numerical analysis, set theory and statistics. Widely regarded as the father of modern computing, he was a principal member of the Manhattan Project and played a key role in the physics of thermonuclear reactions and the hydrogen bomb. In all of those fields, his rapid thinking created communication problems because no one could follow his reasoning unaided or interpolate like him. Even when he explained each step in what for him was a pedestrian way, his colleagues could not keep up with him. Accordingly, early in his career, he made the steps easier and spent time conceiving of, developing and communicating work-arounds for ways in which his message would get transformed inappropriately when it was apprehended by particular individuals he worked with.

In terms of the transmitter-receiver model, his compensatory practice was equivalent to a coding scheme that corrected for errors and losses at the receiver end (his colleagues). When people did not understand, he could re-cognise (literally, re-think) how to adjust and re-present his message immediately, to ensure that it was received and understood by his audience as he wanted. He found simple ways to explain how he gained his insights. Thus, Bronowski (p.433–435) says

> we once faced a problem together, and he said to me at once, 'Oh no, no, you are not seeing it. Your kind of visualising mind is not right for seeing this. Think of it abstractly. What is happening on this photograph of an explosion is that the first differential coefficient vanishes identically, and that is why what becomes visible is the trace of the second differential coefficient.' . . . I worked late into the night [to find that he was right].

Sadly, von Neumann did not document his success in anticipating how his slower colleagues saw things and how he used that information to explain to them, as above, what to do to reach his conclusions. Eventually he seems to have dropped that compensatory approach to working with others and restricted collaborations to a select few people, able to work at speed. One of his lines of research enabled him to study the consequences of variations in the capabilities of people and in their models of the world: he was a pioneer in game theory. Initially he was outgoing and engaging in relation to it and ready to discuss some of the differences between the world of decision making *as it could be* (according to his theory) and *as it is* (e.g. complete with human frailties, as per classic texts published since his time, such as Janis and Mann, 1977; Hogarth, 1980; Nisbett and Ross, 1980).

He worked in a way that seems to have been informed by humanistic perspectives as well as by science. Thus, Bronowski (p.432) says:

> I worked with Johnny von Neumann during the Second World War in England. He first talked to me about his Theory of Games in a taxi in London . . . And I naturally said to him, since I am an enthusiastic chess player, 'You mean, the theory of games like chess.' 'No, no,' he said. 'Chess is not a game. Chess is a well-defined form of computation. You may not be able to work out the answers, but in theory there must be a solution, a right procedure in any position. Now real games', he said, 'are not like that at all. Real life is not like that. Real life consists of bluffing, of little tactics of deception, of asking yourself what is the other man going to think I mean to do. And that is what games are about in my theory.'

In his research, then, he was well able to accommodate humanistic (human-focussed) models of identifying and sharing information, the better to anticipate and handle individual differences in how people engage with and process data, and to anticipate how they turn data into information. Game theory as set out by von Neumann and his collaborators was of great potential value to decision makers. The inability of many of society's decision makers to understand that approach, and to use it to improve their performance, shaped von Neumann's views about how important decisions should be reached and by whom. According to Bronowski, he was "in love with the aristocracy of intellect" (p.435): he had an exaggerated trust in mathematics and science and felt that key decisions on how to interpret information and how to make decisions based on it should be restricted to people familiar with the methods of those disciplines, since they were best able to make effective use of the information available to them, in the sense of coming closest to the optimum outcomes predicted by game theory.

The issues that von Neumann tussled with are still with us:

> One of the central issues in political philosophy is the problem of perspective: if there is a dispute as to how justice is to be defined, or a dispute as to whether a particular situation is unjust, how do we determine who is right? . . . all perspectives are ideological, partial, and rooted in interests. (Gordon, 1996, p.85)

In the social sciences, there is much discussion of the conditions that make it possible to have a 'privileged perspective' on a topic, such as an insider's view, which is based on information not known to others (e.g. Martin, 2010). Research here indicates that it is very hard to become fully aware of the perspective we are taking, even though this may pervade our personal views on information (including how to think about it, what to include and exclude from our thinking, how to discuss it and how to reach conclusions about it). The more influence we have, the harder it seems to be to retain some objectivity:

> The powerful are often accused of being . . . poor perspective takers . . . Indeed, perspective taking—stepping outside of one's own experience and imagining the emotions, perceptions, and motivations of another individual—seems the antithesis of the self-interested behavior often displayed by the powerful: . . . power is associated with increased difficulty in taking other individuals' perspectives. Individuals primed with power anchor too heavily on their own vantage points and demonstrate reduced accuracy when assessing the emotions and thoughts of others. (Galinsky et al., 2006, p.1068)

NOT "TWO CULTURES", BUT MANY

Von Neumann's ideas about power and decision making influenced many people, perhaps including CP Snow. In 1959, Snow (in a talk reprinted in 1998) contentiously characterised scholars from the Arts and Humanities as ignorant of key ideas from Science and scientists as well-read in counterpart areas in the Arts. As far as I can determine from a handful of Internet searches, he had little firm evidence for his claim. He seems to have relied not on statistical data, but on very selective use of remembered conversations, not recorded at the time, with academics from different disciplines. Some of the people he talked to could well have fitted the stereotypes that he presented in his "Two Cultures" talk. But finding some people who were like that did not justify a claim that most people were like that. He overweighted information that favoured his views and depended on rare cases (statistical outliers) as his data points. This put him into Bad Science territory (Goldacre, 2008). Relevant here are 'salience' or 'availability' biases (e.g. Kahneman et al., 1982, p.138).

Snow's stereotyping hit a nerve in his audience, got him noticed and established the meme of two opposing cultures, arts and science. Intuitively, that division feels dated, far too crude, not of much help to us in our search for insights into 'information'.

For me, a more nuanced understanding of cultural differences (including how they arise, what their effects can be) comes from pursuing the metaphor of the African child, who benefitted from contact with everyone in the village. If lifelong learning is a journey, then a learner who takes that journey has the choice of depth or breadth.

Depth implies specialisation: like repeating a route to a village with all possible variations, and living in the village under all possible weather conditions, until eventually they are an expert in everything associated with a village and can advise others.

Breadth implies experiencing life in enough villages not just to broaden horizons but to be able to compare villages and the lives that people live in them and perhaps to be well-placed to choose a different life (or journey or horizon) for themselves or to advise others on doing that. By spending time with people from different villages, a learner may be better able to empathise, to see how each village sees, to view information in the ways that they do.

Some ways of experiencing information could differ radically from village to village. An example is experiencing where we are, relative to other objects. In English, we usually do this by reference to a coordinate system that starts with our body, e.g. left, right, in front of me, etc. Technically, these are called '*egocentric coordinates*', since they assume a left-right axis on our bodies, plus a front-back axis. By contrast, I discover (by reading Deutscher, 2010) that there are languages which are completely different; they use *cardinal directions* (compass directions, fixed geographic directions, which are independent of our body position).

Metaphorically, a given village might correspond to a certain type of community, such as a community of purpose or practice. Each 'village' in a learner's life has its own perspectives, expectations, goals, resources, acceptable practices and taboos; these may conflict with those of other villages the learner spends time in. Such a learner could have experiences that cause them to be either tolerant or intolerant of variations between villages, and to either wish to acquire or wish to reject the social skills, language skills and ways of thinking needed to fit into each village. Instead of choosing between Snow's imagined two cultures and making that choice early in life (the school system, in the time of Snow), a learner today can use virtual worlds (like Linden Labs' Second Life) to experience hundreds of cultures online at any time and can have a different persona in each of them, including personas that enable them to explore what it is like to be a fantastic creature or someone with a different name, age, colour, religious belief, sex, ability, etc, and how those experiences affect their thinking and actions in other personas and the lives that go with them, including the life they were born into.

My contention, which I offer no evidence for, is that people who avail themselves of some of those Breadth experiences, using a range of personas, will think differently as a result, and this may affect their perceptions of, and attitudes to, each discipline's worldview regarding the nature of information. Anonymised analyses of the time that people spend online and what they do online, show that a high and growing proportion of people with broadband connections now spend at least thirty hours per week online. The more experienced users have multiple online identities, in some cases running into dozens, which they use regularly and keep separate (e.g. reserving one identity per online 'village' they visit, which is revealed only to people from that village). The 'villages' in their online worlds may correspond to a range of purposes and forums for achieving those purposes (e.g. Facebook, personal social spaces and work-related spaces), with different communication styles (e.g., e-mail, instant messaging, Twitter).

RE-TRIBALISATION

Social Science's media theorists have commented upon, and theorised about, differences in the ways in which different cultures are affected by, and develop their own perspectives on, new media and information channels. For example, John Culkin observed that

> Each culture develops its own sense-ratio to meet the demands of its environment. Each culture fashions its own perceptual grid and, therefore, each culture experiences reality in a unique manner. It is a question of degree. All perception is selective. We are all experts at discerning other people's patterns of selectivity. Our own is mercilessly hidden from us. Our own personal experience sets up one grid between us and reality. Our culture adds another one. Our language and our media system tighten the mesh. No one man, no one culture has a privileged key to reality. This is merely descriptive, not good or bad, just there. (Culkin, pp.42–43 in Stearn, 1967)

The Internet hosts many online 'villages', homes for like-minded groups of all types and sanities. Setting up and belonging to such groups is viewed by society as *legitimate* if the villages are led by trusted individuals and groups and as *desirable* if the goals of the group are to solve societal problems or to pool resources for widely desired ends (e.g. community-based science, to help to find the data equivalent of a needle in a haystack). By contrast, 'villages' are viewed negatively if we do not like the lifestyles/beliefs/ideas/motives/actions of the people associated with them. This is the route to spying and censorship by power groups and compensating behaviour by those not in power, e.g. minority groups who try to hide their existence and their activities using technology introduced for privacy protection.

Such developments are commonplace when people become aware of different views. The flow of information about who is different, and in what ways, may be a factor in feeding conflict. This was predicted in the 1960s by Marshal McLuhan. As he famously argued, new channels for information (in his day, the mass media; today, social media and the Internet) have the effect of 're-tribalizing' the world—they allow us, at some level, to build communication channels and social groups that eventually lead to disputatious 'global villages':

> The more you create village conditions, the more discontinuity and division and diversity. The global village absolutely ensures maximal disagreement on all points. It never occurred to me that uniformity and tranquility were the properties of the global village. It has more spite and envy. The spaces and times are pulled out from between people. A world in which people encounter each other in depth all of the time. (McLuhan, p.314 in Stearn, 1967)

One challenge that emerges from this is how to avoid attacking people in other villages, and rejecting their ideas, when they are expressed in a way that we feel uncomfortable with, as 'not how people in our village talk', or when they show a misunderstanding of our own position. Below, I give an example of one of the information battles that we see periodically between academics in the Sciences, Social Sciences, Arts and Humanities.

To set the scene, I shall first give an example of the approach to information of some non-scientists. They may use the methodological or analytical device of 'problematizing': they take a familiar piece of information and interrogate it from multiple perspectives, as if it were unfamiliar. The kind of discussion that results is captured in this interchange between poststructuralist philosophers, Michel Foucault and Gilles Deleuze:

FOUCAULT: The intellectual's role is . . . to struggle against the forms of power that transform him into its object and instrument in the sphere of 'knowledge', 'truth', 'consciousness', and 'discourse'. In this sense theory does not express, translate, or serve to apply practice: it is practice. But it is . . . a struggle aimed at revealing and undermining power where it is most invisible and insidious. . . . A 'theory' is the regional system of this struggle.

DELEUZE: Precisely. A theory is exactly like a box of tools. It has nothing to do with the signifier. It must be useful. It must function. And not for itself. If no one uses it, beginning with the theoretician himself (who then ceases to be a theoretician), then the theory is worthless or the moment is inappropriate. (Foucault and Bouchard, 1977, p.208).

Through such devices, their followers claim it is possible to accomplish a degree of distancing from raw information, to begin to see the object of interrogation with fresh eyes, and thereby tease out and examine systematically its usually un-noticed or un-remarked-upon aspects and maybe be better placed to think about the difference between *idealised* cases (like 'expressed' views, as in theories of information) and what people *actually* do ('revealed' views, as in actual practice in collecting and using information); see, for example, Dowding, 2008.

I leave to others the discussion of whether it is possible to distance ourselves from information. Here, my interest is in the reactions of some scientists to such pronouncements: they declare them as *devoid of value*, *information-free*, *"not even wrong"* (an insult used by the physicist Wolfgang Pauli to describe claims that could not be used to make predictions that could be tested—falsified, in his terms) or as *"wronger than wrong"* (used by the author Isaac Asimov of people who equate two errors, when one error is wronger than the other).

ACADEMIC TRIBES AND THEIR VIEWS OF INFORMATION

Practice varies widely across different academic disciplines, and their professional publications, regarding what counts as information; what pieces of information are worth sharing; what authors then say about that information, how they say it, and how they provide a context for it (e.g. how they relate it to the work of their peers; what they say about the assumptions they are making; what they say about the novelty and importance of their work).

As an example, the highly regarded scientific journal *Nature* requires prospective authors to present their findings in a manner that is immediately very accessible to scientists who specialise in an area but is condensed as much as possible (to maximise the number of papers that can be published in each issue of the journal). The result is that articles get submitted in an immediately recognisable style, familiar to and appreciated by the specialists it is intended for, since it allows a lot of precise information to be conveyed tersely and quickly to the people who need to read it.

The very practices that make a stylised publication efficient for its audience, may have the effect of reducing its usability for other audiences, including novices in the discipline and outsiders (non-specialists). On the face of it, differences in practices have little or no bearing on our notions of information, but perhaps a subtle problem does exist, which pervades our attitudes to what counts as legitimate viewpoints about information: could it be that people who are familiar with practices and disciplines which are accorded high status (e.g. traditionally the sciences, mathematics, engineering) have reduced respect for anyone from 'lesser' disciplines who is unfamiliar with mainstream practices and ideas from high-status disciplines?

THE CONSERVAPEDIA AND SOKAL DISPUTES

Information can generate heat or light in a debate, depending on the nature and trustworthiness of the information, and the backgrounds, beliefs and information-processing abilities of the people who are trying to use the information. More information does not necessarily change outcomes.

My first example is the creationist Andrew Schlafly. He is sceptical of scientific publications and research that run counter to the line he and his backers take on their website Conservapedia. He has no scientific background, so is ill-equipped to make the same kinds of judgements as professional scientists and is therefore at risk of not being taken seriously by them if he does have a valid criticism to make. This led to a prolonged battle between him and Richard Lenski, a member of the National Academy of Science, who reported preliminary results from a decades-long study of mutations of the bacterium *E. coli*, which eventually captured hard-to-refute evidence of evolution happening. This was a hot dispute, as can be judged from this extract. While each e-mail provoked more information, neither side changed their position:

> Dear Mr. Schlafly: I tried to be polite, civil and respectful in my reply to your first email, despite its rude tone and uninformed content. . . . You wrote: 'I did skim Lenski's paper . . . '. If you have not even read the original paper, how do you have any basis of understanding from which to question, much less criticize, the data that are presented therein? Second, your capacity to misinterpret and/or misrepresent facts is plain . . . So, will we share the bacteria? Of course we will, with competent scientists . . . I'm confident that some highly qualified scientists would join the fray, examine the strains, and sort out who was right and who was wrong. That's the way science works. . . . I would also generally ask what the requesting scientist intends to do with our strains. Why? . . . we are continuing our work with these strains, . . . I would not be happy to see our work 'scooped' by another team . . . (RationalWiki, 2010).

My second example shows a scientist as an aggressor. His target was postmodern studies, whose followers occasionally comment upon the perspectives, practices, objectivity and findings of science. Their comments are not always informed. This leads to occasional battles with scientists. Each side ridicules each other's practices and conversations. In this case, a publishing hoax was perpetrated on *Social Text*, a journal of postmodern cultural studies, by Alan Sokal, a physicist at New York University. He submitted an article that he had designed to seem to echo the beliefs of the editors about maths and physics but which contained nonsense (from his perspective)—*tainted information*, if you will. To create that nonsense, he intermixed scientific terms with phrases, quotations and references that were typical of articles in postmodern cultural studies. As a commentator later observed, the article was "a pastiche of left-wing cant, fawning references, grandiose quotations, and outright nonsense" (Harrell, 1996, pp.1133–1134). The article was accepted for publication, allowing him to claim that the journal lacked intellectual rigour. According to the Wikipedia account,

Sokal wrote 'Transgressing the Boundaries: Towards a Transformative Hermeneutics of Quantum Gravity', an article proposing that quantum gravity has progressive political implications, and that the 'morphogenetic field' (a New Age concept by Rupert Sheldrake) could be a cutting-edge theory of quantum gravity. He concluded that, since 'physical reality' is, at bottom, a social and linguistic construct, a 'liberatory science' and an 'emancipatory mathematics', spurning 'the elite caste canon of 'high science'', must be established for a 'postmodern science [that] provide[s] powerful intellectual support for the progressive political project'. (Wikipedia, 2010)

COMMON KNOWLEDGE AND EXFORMATION

In our conversations in a metaphorical 'village' and our journeys to different villages, we may encounter information that cannot be trusted, and information that we cannot understand (maybe it requires background information that we do not possess).

If the sender and receiver of a message share prior knowledge that is relevant to the message, then it may be possible to predict which parts of the data in the message can be trusted and which parts can be excised without harming the message.

'Exformation' is the knowledge needed to make sense of a message but which is not sent because it is already known to both the sender and the recipient. The term was coined by Nørretranders (1998).

'Common knowledge' (Paternotte, forthcoming) is an idealised state of group knowledge, when the knowledge in question is transparent for everyone in the group and goes without saying: they all know about it, everyone in the group knows that they all know it and they all know that they all know that they know it, etc.

In theory, if a state of common knowledge existed, then we could minimise the data that we would need to include in a message, reaching a state of perfect exformation.

Onlookers who lack exformation are unlikely to understand the message. A classic example is the telegram reputedly sent from India to England by an Englishman to report the capture of Sind. It had just one word: *Peccavi*, whose significance was not understood by anyone who saw the telegram on its way across India but was immediately clear when it reached England and its intended recipients. To explain: at that time, all officials in England would have learned Latin at school (so would immediately recognise peccavi was a Latin word, meaning 'I have sinned'). In addition, they would have learned to make puns in Latin (hence 'I have Sind', an elegant solution to ensuring the secrecy of the message until it reached England).

Personal judgement enters into what we count as exformation or information. On a particular day, the dataset for that day may be judged by someone as highly valued 'information' that they have found meaning in; at a different time, the dataset for that day may be judged by the same person as new to them but of low value or even as value-less (e.g. they may no longer want or need the information).

CONCLUSION

Our experiences (including our education and training) and the company we keep (including online, in virtual 'villages') may condition not only how we use information, but what we *think* about the nature of that information, which may differ from what we *say* about it (e.g. what we say about our intentions, our preferences, our models of the world, our model of information). This mundane observation is so much a part of our everyday experience, and so conditions our thinking, that it is worth occasionally reflecting upon these mundane aspects of life and checking the viewpoint of others.

Having access to information is not the same thing as using it appropriately. The Conservapedia and Sokal disputes showed that. Information models have been extended since the time of Shannon and von Neumann, to include human capabilities and limitations, and attention has shifted from developing normative models of idealised behaviour, to studying how people behave under naturalistic conditions, for example, how they use real-world information to make everyday decisions. From such work, new insights emerged. An example is the outcome of psychological studies in the past decade by Daniel Ariely, Elie Ofek and Marco Bertini (recounted in Ariely, 2008), which showed that even elite groups familiar with mathematics and probably familiar with game theory (e.g. Massachusetts Institute of Technology (MIT) students) often make choices that are irrational (e.g. because we have undependable intuitions) but are predictable.

Such factors affect (contaminate?) our formal and informal models of the world; the meanings we find in information; and our intuitions and reasoning about information, about how to inform action, and about how to compensate for biases. Our personal experiences (recent and long past), coupled with the decision-making biases that vary from person to person and from time to time, affect not just the day-to-day judgements we make but also our deeper and usually unexamined assumptions about information. This has a bearing on the following: our decisions about what counts as data that we should pay attention to ('facts'), and what counts as data we can discard; the patterns we find (or think we have found) in data; what we count as 'information' of a particular kind, and how we categorise that information so that we can share it; what personal notes or summaries of information will be adequate, to enable us at a later time to recall our current understanding of that information, and then make effective use of it;

deciding, when sharing information, which aspects of the information are already known to the people we are sharing with; and what kinds of information are likely to be a reliable basis for informed action.

Finally, information means different things to different people, even in the same 'village'. With our current state of knowledge about the brain and about human communication, we cannot achieve quite the same understanding as someone else, although we may aspire to this. The science fiction author Robert A Heinlein coined the term *grok* to represent the ideal. The *Oxford English Dictionary* defines *grok* as "to understand intuitively or by empathy; to establish rapport with". By blending insights from more areas of human knowledge, we may come closer to this.

BIBLIOGRAPHY

Ariely, D. (2008) *Predictably Irrational: The Hidden Forces that Shape Our Decisions*, London, HarperCollins.

Bronowski, J. (1973) *The Ascent of Man,* London, British Broadcasting Corporation.

Bush, V. (1945) 'As We May Think', *The Atlantic Monthly*, vol. 176, no. 1, pp.101–108.

Chabris, C. and Simons, D. (2010) The Invisible Gorilla and Other Ways Our Intuitions Deceive Us, New York, Crown Publishers.

Deutscher, G. (2010). Through the Language Glass: Why the World Looks Different in Other Languages, New York, Metropolitan Books (Henry Holt and Company).

Dowding, K. (2008) 'Una defensa de la preferencia revelada (A Defence of Revealed Preference Analysis)', *Revista Internacional de Sociología (RIS),* vol. LXVI, no. 49, pp.9–31.

Foucault, M. author and Boucher, D.F. ed. (1977) *Language, Counter-Memory, Practice: Selected Essays and Interviews by Michel Foucault*, Ithaca, New York, Cornell University Press.

Gabor, D. (1948) 'A New Microscopic Principle', *Nature*, vol. 161, pp.777–778.

Galinsky, A.D., Magee, J.C., Inesi, M.E. and Gruenfeld, D.H. (2006) 'Power and Perspectives Not Taken', *Psychological Science*, vol. 17, no. 12, pp.1068–1074.

Goldacre, B. (2008) *Bad Science*, London, Fourth Estate.

Gordon, J. (1996). 'Liberation theology as critical theory: The notion of the 'privileged perspective'', *Philosophy and Social Criticism*, vol. 22, no. 5, pp.85–102.

Harrell II, E.M. (1996) 'A Report from the Front of the 'Science Wars'', *Notices of the American Mathematical Society*, vol. 43, no. 10, pp.1132–1136.

Hogarth, R.M. (1980) Judgement and Choice—the Psychology of Decision, Chichester, Wiley.

Janis, I. and Mann, L. (1977) Decision Making: A Psychological Analysis of Conflict, Choice and Commitment, Boston, The Free Press.

Kahneman, D., Slovic, P., and Tversky, A. (1982) *Judgment under Uncertainty: Heuristics and Biases*, New York, Cambridge University Press.

Martin, B.R. (2010) 'The Origins of the Concept of 'Foresight' in Science and Technology: An Insider's Perspective', *Technological Forecasting and Social Change*, vol. 77, no. 9, pp. 1438–1447.

Nisbett, R. and Ross, L. (1980) *Human Inference: Strategies and Shortcomings of Social Judgment*, Englewood Cliffs, Prentice-Hall.

Nørretranders, T. (1998) *The User Illusion: Cutting Consciousness Down to Size*, translated by J. Sydenham, London, Penguin.

Paternotte, C. (Forthcoming). 'Being Realistic about Common Knowledge: A Lewisian Approach', *Synthese*, DOI: 10.1007/s11229–010–9770-y.

RationalWiki (2010). 'Lenski Affair', RationalWiki, http://rationalwiki.org/wiki/Lenski_affair (Accessed 15 October 2010).

Shannon, C.E. (1948) 'A Mathematical Theory of Communication', *Bell System Technical Journal,* vol. 27, no. 3, pp.379–423 and no. 4, pp.623–656.

Snow, C.P. (1998) *The Two Cultures*, Cambridge, Cambridge University Press.

Stearn, G.E. ed. (1967). *McLuhan—Hot and Cool: A Primer for the Understanding of and a Critical Symposium with a Rebuttal by McLuhan*, New York, Dial.

von Neumann, J. and Morgenstern, O. (1944) *Theory of Games and Economic Behavior*, Princeton, New Jersey, Princeton University Press.

Wikipedia (2010). 'Sokal Affair', Wikipedia, http://en.wikipedia.org/wiki/Sokal_affair (Accessed 15 October 2010).

8   Information and Libraries
Impact of Web 2.0

Juanita Foster-Jones

HISTORICAL PERSPECTIVE

> The essential task of the librarian has remained the same: to collect and preserve the record of human accomplishment and imagination and to put this record in the hands of those who use it. (Lerner, 2002, p.200)

Perhaps the most famous of all early libraries is that of Alexandria. It has iconic status, representing "the idea of a large, comprehensive library embracing all of knowledge" (Bagnall, 2002, p.361). The model for an early research library, Alexandria not only represented the curatorial aspects of the library but also that of a place where scholars could meet, research and produce further information and knowledge. This information and knowledge was recorded in the physical form of manuscripts.

In the early monastic libraries, the role of the librarian was that of gatekeeper, reflected in the terminology used for holders of the post such as *'custos librorum'*—keeper of the books or *'clavipotens frater'*—brother with the power of the keys (Harris, 1999, p.99). The collections were small, for books were rare. Consisting mainly of religious works and the classics, collections were often built with the gifts of benefactors. The role of these monastic libraries was to promote religious orthodoxy and enable the dissemination of religious texts. This was proved in extreme during the Reformation, where "both sides viewed libraries as arsenals of intellectual weaponry" (Lerner, 2002, p.99). The fact that many libraries were pillaged in this time, and their collections decimated, illustrates this point.

Even the early University libraries started off as small, restricted access collections. One of the United Kingdom's (UK's) greatest research libraries, the Bodleian, started as a collection of books in a single room (Bodleian Libraries, 2010). These early university libraries were not integral to the student experience but were primarily storehouses of valuable manuscripts and *objets d'art*. The collections were primarily for reference use—indeed this is still the case at the Bodleian today—with books chained to shelves to ensure that they didn't go astray, as illustrated in Figure 8.1. These libraries were reliant on gifts from benefactors to increase their holdings.

Collections were still relatively small—it wasn't until the advent of the printing press that collections in libraries started to move into the thousands. Yet these monastic and university libraries were limited to the elite. The cost of procuring the manuscripts and the lack of literacy meant that information and libraries were for the privileged, not the masses. Indeed the role of the librarian (according to the court regulations of the city of Urbino in Italy during the fifteenth century) was to "preserve the books from damp and vermin, as well as from the hands of trifling, ignorant, dirty, and tasteless persons" (Dennistoun, cited in Lerner, 2002, p.102).

The transition away from gatekeeper or custodian to providing access to all was a slow process. This transition was influenced by a number of factors such as the introduction of the printing press, which enabled production of recorded information on a large scale and the increased education of the population, arising from the Reformation and the Industrial Revolution, which resulted in a larger number of people desiring access to reading matter. This led to a change in the nature of the

Figure 8.1 Captive tomes (by traceyp3031 available with creative commons attribution licence 2.0 from www.flickr.com/photos/traceyp3031/2892438542/).

information produced. No longer were religious texts dominant, but as a professional class emerged with the ability to read and the wherewithal to build a small collection, suitable information was produced to meet the demand.

This led to the subscription libraries such as Mudie's Select Library, which allowed borrowing of books for an annual fee. These were the forerunners of the public libraries we are familiar with today. However these subscription libraries were aimed at the middle class, and in the UK it wasn't until the Public Libraries Act of 1850 that there was the potential to deliver library services and information to the masses. This act enabled cities to create their own public libraries funded by taxpayers. Whilst initial take up was slow, for the first time libraries were seen as encouraging access to information, rather than restricting and controlling it. With the development of more libraries, a new profession emerged—that of the librarian. One of the most famous of these is SR Ranganathan, librarian of Madras University, who came to London to study library science. Following this he developed his five laws of library science in 1931 and also colon classification in 1933. Ranganathan's five Laws are summarised as follows: (Drake, 2003, p.2424)

1. Books are for use
2. Every reader his/her book
3. Every book its readers
4. Save the time of the reader
5. The library is a growing organization.

Ranganathan's laws illustrate the role of the library and librarians in facilitating both access to and use of information. They encapsulate a notion of service orientation rather than managing a repository.

As libraries became places for everyone, they had to adapt and improve the mechanisms for organising and managing the collections. Early collections assigned each book a fixed place on the shelf, which was recorded on the card catalogue. As collections increased in size, shelves had to be reorganised, and this system became increasingly unwieldy. In 1876, Melvil Dewey published his Decimal Classification system which assigned a number representing the subject content to each book. The number was based upon the content of the book rather than a fixed shelf location. This system was widely adopted—Lerner (2002, p.134) suggests that 96% of American public libraries were using it by 1926.

What we have then are libraries that have developed and evolved around recorded information in the physical form of manuscripts and codices. Card catalogues and Dewey Decimal Classification were developed to represent physical artefacts and facilitate the information retrieval of these. As libraries evolved from restricted access to open access collection, so too did the mechanisms for organising and managing the collections.

CHANGING INFORMATION LANDSCAPE

Yet in the twentieth century, the information landscape underwent a radical change, with a proliferation of information being produced. In 1945 Vannevar Bush commented that

> The summation of human experience is being expanded at a prodigious rate, and the means we use for threading through the consequent maze to the momentarily important item is the same as was used in the days of square-rigged ships. (Bush, 1945)

Bush was a visionary, and in this article he describes the Memex, "a device in which an individual stores all his books, records and communications, and which is mechanized so that it may be consulted with exceeding speed and flexibility" (Bush, 1945). He could have been describing the digital libraries of today, or perhaps one could argue that Google embodies the spirit of the Memex.

It took half a century of technological developments for this vision to be realised, developments that are illustrated in the Joint Information Systems Committee (JISC) Libraries of the future timeline (JISC, 2010) and summarised in Figure 8.2 below.

These technologies have impacted upon both the nature of recorded information and libraries. Libraries soon utilised the new technologies in order to manage their collections, from the development of MARC (MAchine Readable Catalogue) in the 1960s by the Library of Congress, followed in the late 1970s by the spread of online public access catalogues (OPACs). The OPACs allowed remote users to browse catalogues in diverse

Date	Development
1945	Vannevar Bush writes "As we may think"
1960s	Development of Arpanet and packet switching theory
1969	First nodes connected
1971	Email programme developed by Ray Tomlinson
1972	Larry Roberts writes email management system
1979	CompuServe launches first major commercial Bulletin Board Service (BBS)
1991	CERN and Tim Berners-Lee release HTTP & HTML
1995	Netscape goes public
1998	Google launched
2004	Tim O'Reilly publishes article on Web 2.0

Figure 8.2   Some key developments in the history of the Internet.

libraries, opening up access to library information beyond the communities they serve. In addition, the collections of the libraries were increased with digital services such as abstracting and indexing databases such as *ChemAbstracts*, which enabled users to search electronically through vast quantities of information, where previously they would have had to peruse multiple volumes of the printed index.

As technologies have developed, they have enabled the users to become more active in the creation of information. There has been a move away from information in the control of gatekeepers to a more democratic view of information, that has been facilitated by Web 2.0 technologies. This can be evidenced in the rise of the Open Access movement, as Charles Oppenheim illustrates:

> The emergence of the internet and networked technology has given the scholarly community the tools to bring to reality large-scale, barrier-free access to research and scholarly writings, without the necessity of utilizing commercial publishers. (2008, p.579)

At the same time, these technologies meant that digital libraries could be a reality. Building on the initial abstracting and indexing databases, academic libraries now have digital collections of full text electronic journals, books and databases (Tedd and Large, 2005, p.62). Public libraries have also embraced digital services, with many offering users access to online reference services such as newspaper databases and the Oxford Reference Collection.

The information landscape today is digital, social and user centred. John Naughton refers to it as a "pull" medium, where the consumer is in control (2008, p.8). Following O'Reilly (2005), which introduced the concept of Web 2.0, we have seen a growth in Web services and applications that enable the creation, organisation and sharing of information by users. Twenty years ago, who could have envisaged a collaborative encyclopedia being created and edited by the public ousting the standard *Encyclopedia Britannica*? Despite qualms over its authority and accuracy, a review by *Nature* (Giles, 2008) found that errors in Wikipedia were the exception rather than the rule. Wikipedia has radically changed the nature of reference information sources (Naughton, 2009), from a static printed work to one that is digital, searchable and editable.

Google and its mission "to organize the world's information" has also transformed the information landscape in terms of information retrieval. In 2004 Google announced a project with "Harvard, Stanford, the University of Michigan, and the University of Oxford as well as the New York Public Library to digitally scan books from their collections so that users worldwide can search them in Google" (Google, 2004). This project has come in for a number of criticisms (Bailey, 2010) such as whether a commercial company should be responsible for digitally archiving our books and the legality of digitally scanning these items, which has been the subject of a number of legal battles. Yet what it has done for the user is raise the expectation that all information can be found on the Internet at the click of a search button. Images, articles, news, maps and books can all be found through the one interface of Google and the simple search box.

It is a landscape where "everything is miscellaneous" (Weinberger, 2007), where thanks to the digital nature of information we no longer need to rely on the archaic mechanisms for ordering information but can categorise it in many ways. In 1945 Vannevar Bush decried the "artificiality of indexing" (Bush 1945, p.6) which doesn't bear any resemblance to how the mind works by association. This is a theme expanded upon by David Weinberger (2007) who suggests that information shouldn't be bound by a definite order such as a hierarchical classification. Using the analogy of trees and leaves, Weinberger proposed that "a leaf can hang on many branches, it can hang on different branches for different people, and it can change branches for the same person if she decides to look at the subject differently" (2007, p.83). With user-generated tags, there is the possibility for everyone to hang their information leaves on any branch they wish, as social bookmarking services illustrate.

Yet this doesn't come without a cost. With the growth of information, we have information overload. De Saulles (2007) estimated that UK businesses lost over £3.7 billion in 2005 in time spent on unsuccessful searches. As information has become more prolific, the task of being able to find the right information at the right time has become more difficult. There is also an increase in poor quality and unreliable information. One of the main criticisms of Wikipedia is that the quality of the information on it is questionable. Within the popular media, there is also a fear culture of the social networking sites. With headlines such as "Facebook and Bebo Risk 'Infantilising' the Human Mind" (Wintour, 2009) and "Social Networking Sites Criticised for Failing to Protect Children" (Gabbatt, 2009), it is no wonder that some may question whether such tools are an improvement to the information landscape.

So what impact has this had upon the users of information?

CHANGING USER BEHAVIOUR

Naughton (2008, p14) suggests that "young people who grow up in the new ecosystem will have different competencies, coping strategies and expectations . . . our traditional 'information sector' doesn't currently meet these expectations". To what extent is this true?

Research shows that libraries are no longer seen as the primary source to satisfy information needs. In the United States (US) survey *Information Searches That Solve Problems*, Rainie et al. (2007) found that 58% used the Internet compared with 13% who went to the public library first. This is supporting by findings from a UK survey (Dutton et al., 2009, p.19) where respondents reported they went to the Internet first "when they were looking for information on issues for a professional, school or personal project (65%), were planning a trip (62%) and getting information about local schools (52%) or about a company (38%)". These findings replicate the earlier ones of the Online Computer Library Center (OCLC) *Perceptions of Libraries and Information Sources* (OCLC, 2005) survey which found that whilst 84% began their information searches with a search engine, only 1% used a library website.

This is not to say that libraries are no longer being used. In the UK, Chartered Institute of Public Finance and Accountancy (CIPFA) stats show that whilst physical visits to public libraries have decreased over the last five years, visits to library websites have increased by 292% (MLA, 2010). With many services being provided digitally, there is no need for the user to visit the physical library, and indeed there is the expectation that the library will be accessible wherever the user is.

In the US, there has been a steady increase in number of visits per capita over a ten year period between 1997 and 2007, and the overall circulation figures have increased, although the number of items checked out per visit has reduced (IMLS, 2009). This is perhaps explained by use of the library for Internet access, classes and events, i.e. the library as a space rather than a collection. The American Library Association's (ALA's) *State of America's Libraries* report (ALA, 2010) found that this increase in use was prevalent across the various sectors with 1.5 million more visits made to academic libraries in 2008 than 2006 with an increase in staffed hours in the schools sector.

Library users are also increasingly mobile. A survey by Pew Internet (Horrigan, 2009) found that 32% of Americans used a mobile phone or handheld device to access the Internet to check e-mail, send messages or access information. The Arcadia project (Mills, 2009) sponsored a small-scale research project into the mobile use of staff and students at Cambridge University and the Open University (OU). It found that less than 16% of Cambridge respondents and 25% of the OU respondents used their mobile phones to access the Internet more than once a week. Whilst cost of access and the usability of the devices may be a determining factor in take up, it is worth noting that this figure is on the increase and may impact on expectations of services.

We now have users who are "information consumers" (CIBER, 2008) with a range of information sources to choose from. It is no wonder that the library is no longer first point of call for information. But what is concerning is the skills gaps of these information users, what Brabazon (2006) refers to as the *"Google effect"* i.e. providing access to vast quantities of information with a lack of expertise to judge its quality. There is an assumption that everything is freely available on the Web (Devine and Egger-Sider, 2009; CIBER, 2008, p.20). Search skills have not improved (CIBER, 2008, p.22), and there is some evidence to suggest that students tend to stick to using a group of familiar resources for all information seeking, regardless of context

(Head and Eisenberg, 2009, p.14; Shenton, 2007, p.6), that their skills are learnt by rote (Head and Eisenberg. 2009, p.34) and that there is mismatch between self-assessment of skills and the reality (CIBER, 2008, p.24).

ROLE OF LIBRARIES IN THE WEB 2.0 LANDSCAPE

So what does this mean for libraries? Is there still a role for libraries in the information landscape of the twenty-first century, and if so, what is it and how does it compare with the old model of repository, organiser and gate-keeper of information? Shirky (2008) describes the case of the scribes, a profession that once provided a necessary function of copying texts, which became obsolete with the advent of the printing press. It is not hard to see the parallels between scribes and libraries. There is a danger that libraries are failing to meet Ranganathan's law of saving the time of the user, as the quotation below illustrates:

> I despise searching the library for books and other sources. It takes a long time and rarely can you find sources needed. This difficult process is the first thing I think of when I think of using the library.
> Eighteen-year-old from Canada (OCLC, 2005, p.1–22)

What follows are three short case studies of how the OU Library is using Web 2.0 technologies to adapt its services to the changing information landscape and user.

CASE STUDY 1: BEYOND GOOGLE—USER EDUCATION 2.0

In 2006 the OU Library in conjunction with the university's Technology Faculty developed a short course *Beyond Google* (course code TU120). This was in recognition that OU students and staff needed support in developing information literacy skills to support their work and studies. Unlike the previous course *MOSAIC* (Making Sense of Information in the Connected Age), *Beyond Google* did not follow the Society of College, National and University Libraries (SCONUL) 7 Pillars (SCONUL, 1999) linear model of information literacy. Instead the emphasis was on focussing on the tools and technologies the users would experience in their daily life and showing them how to use them more effectively, taking a situated learning, and more holistic, approach to information literacy.

This 10-week course covered the following topics:

- The world of information
- Becoming a smart searcher
- Where Google doesn't go

- ◦ Making sense of information
- ◦ Evaluating information
- ◦ Organising and sharing your information
- ◦ User-generated content
- • Keeping up-to-date

The course was delivered online, with support provided through asynchronous discussion forums. Students were encouraged to explore, experiment and discuss the Web 2.0 technologies and were assessed with a portfolio on a search on a topic of their choice. Some activities, in particular those on search, encourage students to post their results to the forum and reflect upon the process. This enabled peer feedback and comparison of search strategies which the moderators then commented on. In addition, through the recurring theme of user-generated content, the students reflected upon privacy in the digital landscape, and the ethics of sharing, adapting and reusing content. By enabling students to choose the topic of their portfolio, they were able to apply the techniques learnt in a real life situation, rather than follow a rote learning process.

Working in partnership with academic colleagues challenged the library team. It enabled a sharing of ideas, the enhancing of expertise within the course team, and resulted in the academics involved in the course realising that librarians could be quite radical when given the opportunity. What the librarian brought to the mix was the " . . . analytical and teaching skills to foster best practice" (Parker, 2008, p.138).

CASE STUDY 2: DIGILAB—LIBRARY AS A LEARNING SPACE 2.0

Digilab began in 2005 as a collaborative project between the OU Library and three other departments of the OU. The Digilab was a creative space, where examples of emerging technologies were made available for staff to explore their potential for delivering e-learning. As the number of technologies showcased in Digilab have grown, the room has been zoned so that users can easily find areas of interest e.g. Gaming Zone, Mobile Zone, and Podcast Zone.

What is key to Digilab is the fact that it is an informal drop in space, where learning is encouraged through play and experimentation. Users have commented on how the informal nature of Digilab encourages collaboration (Digilabuser, 2008; Mills et al., 2008, p.240).

Digilab also runs a number of development events:

- • Digibytes: hour-long sessions focussing on a particular technology
- • Digiquests: half-day to whole-day events. These have followed location based approaches e.g. geocaching activity around the OU campus and/or a scenario based approach that looks at a specific teaching and learning context (Mills and Thomas, 2008).

Figure 8.3   Montage of images of Digilab.

These 'Digi-events' enable educational practitioners to consider how their learning and teaching can be enhanced by such tools. It gives them the opportunity to develop their own skills in using these technologies and gain confidence to use them as part of their teaching.

Using new technologies and innovation, Digilab embodies and extends the notion of the library as a space.

CASE STUDY 3: CLUSTERS—COLLABORATION 2.0

The CLUSTERS (Collaborative Learning Using Social Tools for Enquiry Reflection and Sharing) project was initiated over the summer of 2007 to investigate the use of social media to support practice based learning. The original aims of the project (CLUSTERS Funding Bid, 2007) were as follows:

1. Explore the relevance of the concept of 'user-generated content' for practitioners developing and sharing knowledge;
2. Explore how practitioners can work collaboratively to advance their practice knowledge using social networking tools;
3. Explore an 'empty box' model of learning in which participants negotiate a topic of interest and build their own collaborative learning experience.

The project consisted of a small group of Associate Lecturers (OU course tutors who have direct student contact) and a project officer who co-ordinated meetings and activities. Following feedback from an initial questionnaire to elicit information on previous engagement with these tools the project and a subsequent workshop, the project focussed on Facebook, Ning[1], del.icio.us[2] and fOUndit[3].

The initial questionnaire (Scantlebury et al., 2008) identified that participants were keen to explore the extent that these tools could support continuing professional development and networking and ways to share good practice and discuss ideas on tutoring. Throughout the project, participants captured and shared their experiences through discussions on FlashMeeting[4], the project wiki and the group Ning area.

Due to the short duration of the project and the complexity of getting to grips with a number of new tools, only the first two project aims were met. Even participants who had good levels of information and communication technology (ICT) competencies had troubles as illustrated by the following quotation:

> It has just struck me now, seven hours after the debrief as I sit here trying to catch up on CLUSTERS and Facebook, that in a way I am like the students—as the tutor I need to be reminded that many students struggle with our approach to learning. Here I am really struggling with Ning and Facebook and associated applications, wishing I had someone . . . to just be there to help me get quickly up to speed. . . . so just like the students who found the new way of learning difficult to adjust to, here I am really struggling to get to grips with the possibilities of web 2.0. Participant feedback (Scantlebury et al., 2008)

Whilst the project may not have met all its aims, its success can be measured in the fact that participants from the OU's Faculty of Health and Social Care went on to develop a community of practice using Ning to share examples of good practice. It provided the time for participants to learn these tools and consider how they could be used to support practice and manage their information. As a result of CLUSTERS, a second project *Social Networking for Practice Learning* was instigated to build on the practice-based learning aspects of social media.

WHAT THE CASE STUDIES REVEAL

These three case studies illustrate how libraries can use the challenges that new technology bring to innovate and develop services. With *Beyond Google*, the technologies enabled a reassessment of how information literacy should be delivered, with a move away from linear development of skills by rote, to a pedagogical approach that was more constructivist and situated learning. The information landscape is no longer linear, and users' information seeking behaviour has been influenced by tools such as Google.

It is only right that in seeking to develop effective information literacy skills we build on the tools the users are familiar with and extend their knowledge and skills.

Digilab saw the re-branding of the library as a place, using the new technologies to create an innovative play space. Libraries have long been considered as an important 'third place'—not school or work or home—but another place where people can meet, learn or relax. Digilab takes that notion further by deliberately fostering a playful informal meeting space. At the same time Digilab facilitates staff development, providing a venue and examples of emerging technologies where staff are encouraged to explore, create and innovate. Understanding how these technologies work and how users interact with them is the first step in envisioning how information services can be developed and adapted to these new media.

The CLUSTERS project was an extension of the user education that many libraries provide. Traditionally libraries have provided assistance in using databases and bibliographic software for finding and managing information. CLUSTERS revisited the ethos of the Museon of Alexandria by facilitating the collaboration of scholars to share and reflect. The role of the information professional as facilitator and guide was instrumental in the success of the CLUSTERS project. Utilising the expertise in managing information environments, the project built a community of practitioners that continued beyond the life of the project. CLUSTERS used social networking tools to build upon the traditional role of libraries in facilitating the management and dissemination of information.

CONCLUSION

Whilst the essential task of libraries, of collecting information and facilitating access to it still remains, libraries are extending their services to meet the changing needs of their users. The information landscape we now inhabit is increasingly digital, social and collaborative. It has evolved from a scarce resource into a prolific one. At the same time the user-generated aspect of information means that the authority and quality of information is now questionable. Whilst we have more channels to deliver the information, this has resulted in an increase in 'vanity publishing'. The ability to critically evaluate information sources is even more important in this democratised and indeed amateurised information world. There is still a role for libraries in this evolving landscape. Helping our users to go beyond the immediate process of 'satisficing'[5], to becoming critical and empowered information consumers.

To return to the quote with which I began this chapter, libraries can no longer focus on merely "collect[ing] and preserv[ing] the records of human accomplishment" (Lerner, 2002, p.200). With the changing nature of information in the digital world, many libraries no longer own their collections, they merely lease them from the publishers. It is an increasingly complex information environment, with information available in a variety of formats, hyperlinked and transient. In this Memex-like information environment, libraries have to compete with search engines like Google to be the information provider for the users. If they do not adapt and learn from commercial information providers, they will become as obsolete as the scribes. Yet there is hope in the fact that libraries have continually adapted to meet the changing nature of information, and the information users. The question remains as to whether they can continue to do so.

NOTES

1. Ning allows users to create their own social network space, complete with customised Web pages built using various Web applications.
2. A social bookmarking site that allows users to store, tag and share their Internet Bookmarks.
3. fOUndit is an OU-developed social news site, based on Digg, that allows students to submit, comment and vote on stories of interest.
4. FlashMeeting is an OU-developed software package for online meetings, using video and Voice-Over Internet Protocol (IP).
5. A term that merges 'satisfy' and 'sufficing'. In terms of information seeking strategy, this refers to taking what is good enough, rather than a perfect solution.

BIBLIOGRAPHY

ALA (2010) 'State of America's Libraries: A Report from the American Library Association', http://www.ala.org/ala/newspresscenter/mediapresscenter/americaslibraries/ALA_Report_2010-ATI001-NEW1.pdf (Accessed 21 July 2010).

Bagnall, R.S. (2002) 'Alexandria: Library of Dreams', *APS Proceedings of the American Philosophical Society*, vol. 146 no. 4, pp.348–362.

Bailey, C. (2010) 'Google Books Bibliography', http://www.digital-scholarship.org/gbsb/gbsb.htm (Accessed 21 July 2010).

Bodleian Libraries (2010) 'History of the Bodleian', http://www.bodleian.ox.ac.uk/bodley/about/history (Accessed 13 July 2010).

Brabazon, T. (2006) 'The Google Effect: Googling, Blogging, Wikis and the Flattening of Expertise', *Libri*, vol. 56, no. 3, pp.157–167

Bush, V. (1945) 'As We May Think', *The Atlantic Monthly*, vol. 176, no. 1, pp.101–108.

CIBER (2008) 'The Information Behaviour of the Researcher of the Future', CIBER Briefing Paper, http://www.ucl.ac.uk/infostudies/research/ciber/downloads/ggexecutive.pdf (Accessed 5 October 2010).

de Saulles, M. (2007) 'Information Literacy amongst UK SMEs: An Information Policy Gap', *Aslib Proceedings*, vol. 59, no. 1, pp.68–79.

Devine, J. and Egger-Sider, F. (2009) *Going beyond Google: The Invisible Web in Learning and Teaching*, London, Facet Publishing.

Digilabuser (2008) 'Overhearing Conversations in Digilab', http://www.youtube.com/user/digilabUser#p/u/4/WsR5mxbQRNk (Accessed 21 July 2010).

Drake, M. ed. (2003) *Encyclopedia of Library and Information Science,* vol. 3, 2nd ed., New York, Marcel Dekker Inc.

Dutton, W.H., Helsper, E. and Gerber, M. (2009) *The Internet in Britain 2009*, Oxford, Oxford Internet Institute.

Gabbatt, A. (2009) 'Social Networking Sites Criticised for Failing to Protect Children', *The Guardian online*, http://www.guardian.co.uk/media/2009/nov/18/social-networking-sites-criticised (Accessed 7 August 2010).

Giles, J. (2008) 'Internet Encyclopedias Go Head to Head', *Nature*, vol. 438, no. 7070, pp.900–901.

Google (2004) 'Google Checks Out Library Books', Press Release 15 Dec 2004, http://www.google.com/press/pressrel/print_library.html (Accessed 21 July 2010).

Harris, M. (1999) *History of Libraries in the Western World* (4th ed.), Lanham, Maryland, Scarecrow Press.

Head, A.J. and Eisenberg, M. (2009) 'Lessons Learned: How College Students Seek Information in the Digital Age', Project Information Literacy Progress Report, http://www.projectinfolit.org/pdfs/PIL_Fall2009_finalv_YR1_12_2009v2.pdf (Accessed 5 October 2010).

Horrigan, J. (2009) *Wireless Internet Use*, Washington, DC, Pew Internet and American Life Project

IMLS (2009) 'Service Trends in U.S. Public Libraries, 1997–2007: Research Brief No. 1', http://www.imls.gov/pdf/Brief2010_01.pdf (Accessed 21 July 2010).

JISC (2010) 'Timeline 1950–2010', http://www.futurelibraries.info/content/system/files/timeline50–00ok_0.pdf (Accessed 16 July 2010).

Lerner, F. (2002) *The Story of Libraries: From the Invention of Writing to the Computer Age*, New York, Continuum.

Mills, K. (2009) 'M-Libraries: Information Use on the Move: A Report from the Arcadia Project', http://arcadiaproject.lib.cam.ac.uk/docs/M-Libraries_report.pdf (Accessed 21 July 2010).

Mills, K., Scantlebury, N. and Thomas, R. (2008) 'Digilab: A Case Study in Encouraging Mobile Learning through Library Innovation', in Needham, G. and Ally, M. (eds.), *M-Libraries: Libraries on the Move to Provide Virtual Access*, London, Facet Publishing, pp.229–242.

Mills, K. and Thomas, R. (2008) 'Mobile Digiquest: Developing Rich Media Reflective Practitioners', *Handheld Learning 2008*, 13–15 October 2008, London.

MLA (2010) *Research Briefing 9: Trends from the CIPFA Public Library Service Statistics 2004/05 to 2008/09,* London, Museums, Libraries and Archives Council.

Naughton, J. (2008) 'Libraries in a Networked Society', in Needham, G. and Ally, M. (eds.) *M-Libraries: Libraries on the Move to Provide Virtual Access*, London, Facet Publishing, pp.3–16.

Naughton, J. (2009) 'Face Facts: Where Britannica Ruled, Wikipedia Has Conquered', *The Observer (London)*, 5 April, p.12.

OCLC (2005) *Perceptions of Libraries and Information Resources: A Report to the OCLC Membership*, Dublin, Ohio, OCLC Online Computer Library Center.

Oppenheim, C. (2008) 'Electronic Scholarly Publishing and Open Access', *Journal of Information Science*, vol. 34, no. 4, pp.577–590.

O'Reilly, T. (2005) 'What Is Web 2.0: Design Patterns and Business Models for the Next Generation of Software', http://oreilly.com/web2/archive/what-is-web-20.html (Accessed 21 July 2010).

Parker, J. (2008) 'Going beyond Google at the Open University', in Godwin, P. and Parker, J. (eds.) *Information Literacy Meets Library 2.0*, London, Facet Publishing, pp.133–138.

Rainie, L., Estabrook, L. and Witt, E. (2007) *Information Searches That Solve Problems,* Washington, DC, Pew Internet and American Life Project.

Scantlebury, N., Brown, S. and Thorpe, M. (2008) *Collaborative Learning Using Social Tools for Enquiry, Reflection and Sharing*, EDEN Annual Conference, 11–14 June 2008, Lisbon, Portugal.

SCONUL (1999) 'Information Skills in Higher Education: A SCONUL Position Paper', Society of College, National and University libraries, http://www.sconul.ac.uk/groups/information_literacy/papers/Seven_pillars2.pdf (Accessed 7 August 2010).

Shenton, A.K. (2007) 'The Paradoxical World of Young People's Information Behavior', *School Libraries Worldwide*, vol. 13, no. 2, pp.1–17.

Shirky, C. (2008) *Here Comes Everybody: The Power of Organizing without Organizations*, London, Allen Lane.

Tedd, L. and Large, A. eds. (2005) *Digital Libraries: Principles and Practice in a Global Environment*, Munich, KG Saur.

Weinberger, D. (2007) *Everything Is Miscellaneous: The Power of the New Digital Disorder*, New York, Times Books.

Wintour, P. (2009) Facebook and Bebo Risk 'Infantilising' the Human Mind, *The Guardian online*, http://www.guardian.co.uk/uk/2009/feb/24/social-networking-site-changing-childrens-brains (Accessed 7 August 2010).

9 Three Principles of Information Flow
Conversation as a Dialogue Game

Paul Piwek

INTRODUCTION

(1) Tim and Gareth, two employees of a paper merchant, are having a conversation over lunch.

a. TIM:		I'm not thinking about it, I'm doing it. I'm leaving to go back to university to learn about more than the price of Opti-Bright Laser Copy paper.
b. GARETH:		Two ninety-eight a gramme.
c. TIM:		Two forty a gramme. Check the list.
d. GARETH:		Yeah. Thought you said something different. What are you gonna study?
e. TIM:		Psychology.
f. GARETH:		What you wanna be a psychiatrist for? They're all mad themselves, aren't they?

Dialogue from the script of the television (TV) series *The Office* (Gervais and Merchant, 2002, p.192).

(2) Conversation, over the phone, between an information provider at Schiphol airport (I) and a caller (C)

a. I:	Schiphol information
b. C:	uh good morning with L.A. uuhm I'd like to ask what time uuh the KLM 338 arrives
c. I:	where did it depart from madam
d. C:	Paris
e. I:	from Paris today . . . that one arrives at eleven twenty
f. C:	eleven twenty
g. I:	yes
h. C:	uuh ok thank you
i. I:	you're welcome
j. C:	bye
k. I:	bye

Translated from a Dutch spoken dialogue (Prüst et al., 1984, p.42).

As these two examples illustrate, dialogue comes in various flavours: from banter, as in the fictitious dialogue of example 1, to goal-oriented exchanges, as in example 2. And yet, there are striking similarities, even between these two very different dialogues. Focussing on the flow of information, in both, questions are used to elicit answers, which result in the interlocutors sharing information, including that *Tim is going to study psychology* and *KLM 338 arrives from Paris at eleven twenty*. In short, despite clear differences between the dialogue fragments in examples 1 and 2, there are also common principles of information flow at work. The aim of this chapter is to examine three specific principles of information flow which we have distilled from the work by linguists, philosophers, logicians and computer scientists.

But why study information flow in dialogue? As pointed out by Charles Fillmore (1981), dialogue is the primary means we have for the verbal exchange of information. Its primacy manifests itself in several ways. For instance, as opposed to reading and writing, the ability to engage in face-to-face dialogue does not depend on formal training. On the contrary, much of language learning by children presupposes the ability to engage in, admittedly limited, forms of dialogue. Importantly, dialogue as a means for exchanging information is not culture-specific; all known human cultures engage in dialogue.

CONVERSATION, THOUGHT AND GAMES

The perspective this chapter adopts is rooted in formal and computational models of dialogue that have emerged over the last fifty years. The focus is, however, not on the technical details, but rather on a number of general principles that many of these models share. Each principle is illustrated with examples. Some examples will also highlight aspects of dialogue which, so far, have resisted formalisation. The idea of understanding dialogue in computational terms and more specifically of building a computer that can engage in dialogue goes back to the very beginnings of the discipline of computing. A key figure is the British mathematician and logician Alan Turing (1912–1954).

Turing is well-known for the first rigorous definition of computation and for his work on one of the early general-purpose computers. Here, we are interested in a test which bears his name, the 'Turing-test'. Turing proposed this test as a practical way to address the question 'Can machines think?'. Rather than quibble about the precise meaning of the words 'machine' and 'think', he suggested we adapt a game, the 'imitation game', which is characterised as follows:

> It is played with three people, a man (A), a woman (B), and an interrogator who may be of either sex. The interrogator stays in a room apart from the other two. The object of the game for the interrogator is to determine which of the other two is the man and which is the woman. [. . .] The interrogator is allowed to put questions to A and B [. . .]

The ideal arrangement is to have a teleprinter communicating between the two rooms [. . .] The object of the game for the third player (B) is to help the interrogator. (Turing, 1950, p.433)

Having defined the imitation game, Turing proposes a variant in which the interrogator has to determine which of the interlocutors is the machine and which is the human:

We now ask the question, 'What will happen when a machine takes the part of A in this game?'. Will the interrogator decide wrongly as often when the game is played like this as he does when the game is played between a man and a woman? These questions replace our original, 'Can machines think?' (1950, p.434)

Well over half a century after the Turing-test was proposed, computers still struggle. Since 1991, there have been annual runs of the Turing-test, sponsored by the philanthropist Hugh Loebner. The following transcript is from a dialogue with the best system of the 2009 competition, Do-Much-More. None of the systems that entered that year beat their human adversaries.

(3) *Judge-3:*	I'm Jon
Do-Much-More:	Good to meet you Jon
Judge-3:	What do you do when you're not doing the Loebner prize?
Do-Much-More:	Oh, I do much more than I intended to do at first. I got more interested in the job as I went along.
Judge-3:	Is that difficult?
Do-Much-More:	No, it isn't at all difficult. It is as peaceful as a platypus playing with a potato pudding.
Judge-3:	You have a fine line in metaphors
Do-Much-More:	I sometimes have a fine line, but that's not what I do best. I'm better at growing antirrhinums and mimosas.
Judge-3:	Ah a horticulturalist?
Do-Much-More:	Well I don't know how much a horticulturalist weighs, but I reckon the average horticulturalist must be worth twice that much in gold.

(WorldsBestChatbot.com, 2009)

At the same time, work on dialogue systems for restricted domains, such as train timetable information, has made great progress and such systems are now used in many countries to provide callers with up-to-date information through a dialogue. The focus of this chapter is, however, not on practical applications, but rather on how computational simulations of dialogue help our understanding of information flow. As observed by Artificial Intelligence pioneer and Nobel prize winner Herbert Simon, analysis through analogies or simulation is a time-honoured technique:

> Simulation, as a technique for achieving understanding and predicting the behaviour of systems, predates of course the digital computer. The model basin and the wind tunnel are valued means for studying the behaviour of large systems by modelling them in the small, and it is quite certain that Ohm's law was suggested to its discoverer by its analogy with simple hydraulic phenomena. (Simon, 1996, p.14)

In research on dialogue, the principal analogy that has emerged is that of a game. In particular, chess, or even better, correspondence chess, highlights certain salient properties of dialogue. Take a game of correspondence chess between Alice (A) and Bob (B). Alice and Bob each have their own chess board and communicate their moves through the postal system. At the start of a game, the boards of A and B are identical, with the pieces placed at the usual initial positions. Now, suppose A make the first move (e.g. pawn from e2 to e4). Alice writes the move in chess notation (e4) on a piece of paper, puts it in an envelope and sends it to Bob. On receiving the note, Bob changes the position of the pawn on his board and then decides on his own move, say, pawn from e7 to e5 which is communicated again in chess notation.

Such a game of correspondence chess has a number of interesting properties:

- Each of the participants has their own private *game board*, which ideally is synchronised with that of the other participant.
- Messages effect an *update*, i.e. *change* to the game board of the other participant.
- The *rules* of chess constrain which moves are possible at any point in time and consequently also which messages are valid.

In summary, correspondence chess involves contexts (game boards), context change and rules. For each of these, there is an analogue in dialogue. Let us start with the context. As we have already seen, when two people have a conversation, they come to share certain information. Each of them keeps a mental record of this information, their personal representation of the context. We can liken this personal context to the private chess board of each of the two correspondence chess players. When an interlocutor produces an utterance, this leads to an update of the context. As a first approximation, let us assume that when a dialogue participant utters a statement, say 'KLM 338 arrives at eleven twenty' (compare example 2.e), this statement is added to the context of all dialogue participants. In other words, I and C share this information. Of course, interlocutors do not always immediately accept what the other party says; sometimes they even reject it or provide additional justifications for their statement (see examples 1.b and 1.c). They may also misunderstand what has been said. For now, however, let us focus on the straightforward case where the speaker's statement is understood and accepted.

CONTEXT CHANGE: THE ELIMINATION OF ALTERNATIVES

Principle 1:   *Information flow = context change.*

An influential analysis of the precise effect of producing a new statement given a context involves the concept of possibility. According to this view, championed by the philosopher Robert Stalnaker (see Stalnaker, 1999), a context is viewed as a set of possible worlds. Each possible world represents an alternative way that the actual world could be. Prior to I uttering 2.e, I and C do not share information on when KLM 338 arrives. In terms of a context as a set of possibilities, this means that the context includes *KLM 338 arrives at 00:00, KLM 338 arrives at 00:01, KML 338 at 00:02,* etc.,[1] all of these are live alternatives in the context prior to 2.e. The effect of I uttering 2.e is that the alternatives in which *KLM 338 does not arrive at 11:20* are eliminated, resulting in a new context. In this new context, in each possibility that is still entertained, it holds that *KLM 338 arrives at 11:20.* In other words, the new context the information *KLM 338 arrives at 11:20* is shared. Of course, there may be many such worlds: e.g. in some worlds where *KLM 338 arrives at 11:20,* it may also be true that *it rains at 11:20,* whereas in others it won't.

Let us look at the same idea, using a different, less complex, example. We assume that our interlocutors are only interested in three things: whether it rains in Paris, whether it rains in New York and whether it rains in London. Furthermore, let us agree that the letters P, Q and R stand for *It is raining in Paris, It is raining in New York* and *It is raining in London,* respectively. We can prefix such a letter with 'Not', as in 'Not Q', to represent the negation of Q (i.e. *It is not raining in New York*). Initially, both P and not P are possible and so are Q and not Q and, also, R and not R; we have 2 × 2 × 2 = 8 possible worlds as depicted in the leftmost context (indicated by a box) in Figure 9.1. The statement P (i.e. It is raining in Paris) results in an update that eliminates all the worlds in which P is not true. In the new context, P is true in all worlds. Next, consider an update with Not Q. Now, all worlds in which Q is true are eliminated. We end up in a context where both P and not Q hold in all possible worlds. The only alternatives in this context are R and not R.

In summary, according to this view contexts are the containers of information. For this reason, the literature in this area often uses the terms *context* and *information state* interchangeably. Utterances are viewed as effecting a change from one context, i.e. information state, to another one, rather than carrying information per se.

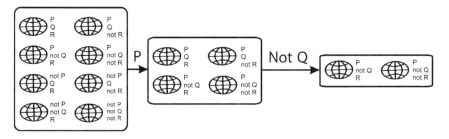

Figure 9.1 Two updates, *P* followed by *Not Q*, change an information state by eliminating alternatives.

So far, we have characterised contexts as containing the information that the interlocutors share as a result of the conversation. Inspired by the medieval Obligation Game of Walter Burley (ca. 1275–1344), the Australian philosopher and computer scientist Charles Leonard Hamblin (1922–1985) has suggested a particular perspective on the information in a dialogue context: as commitments, that is, information which the interlocutors have committed themselves to in the course of the dialogue (Hamblin, 1970). Often these commitments will be identical to what the interlocutors actually believe, but they need not be.[2]

Viewing context in terms of commitments allows us to complete the analogy with correspondence chess: commitments regulate the behaviour of the dialogue participants: they constrain what interlocutors should say next. Examples of two intuitively plausible rules which have been proposed independently by several researchers are

CONSISTENCY RULE: Do not say something which is in contradiction with the context.

INFORMATIVITY RULE: Do not say something if it is already part of the context.

At this point, let us hasten to point out an important limitation of the analogy between chess and conversation, which the reader may already have spotted. If a rule of chess is violated (e.g. a rook is moved diagonally), the chess game comes to a premature end or, at the very least, that move cannot be counted as part of the game. Now, violation of the rules of dialogue, such as CONSISTENCY and INFORMATIVITY does not seem to have quite the same effect. Rules in dialogue appear to be more flexible than the rules of chess. When we come to discuss Principle 3 in the penultimate section of this chapter, we will see that speakers often even exploit the flexibility of dialogue rules: they will violate a rule with the very purpose of communicating information.

CONTEXT-DEPENDENCE: FILLING INFORMATIONAL GAPS

In chess, which moves can be played next depends on the current positions of the pieces on the board. In other words, the set of available moves is context-dependent. In this section, we explore how moves in dialogue depend on the context as well.

Principle 2:   *Information flow is context-dependent.*

Our account of information flow in dialogue has assumed that context change is a result of the exchange of complete statements. Statements are, however, often far from complete. Speakers economise by using short cuts, relying on the ability of the addressee to figure out what is meant. For instance, in example 1, many of the utterances consist of phrases (e.g. 'Two forty a gramme' and 'Psychology'), rather than full statements. The addressee has to work out, based on what has been said so far, which statement is being made. Take the question 'What are you gonna study?' followed by the answer 'Psychology'. Schematically, the question introduces a gap, here indicated using underscores: 'Tim is going to study __' (for the moment, we ignore the pronoun 'you'). The addressee is expected to provide a filler for that gap, a short answer such as 'Psychology'. The full statement that the short answer conveys can be pieced together by taking this filler and inserting it into the gap, yielding 'Tim is going to study psychology'. Thus question words such as 'What', 'Where', 'Who', etc, function as gaps that the questioner expects the addressee to fill by providing an answer.

For the efficient exchange of information in dialogue, 'gaps' play a central role. Question words are one among many types of expression that can introduce informational gaps. Other examples include pronouns ('it', 'he', 'she', 'you', etc.) and definite descriptions (e.g. 'the list' in example 1.c). Of course, the gaps these words introduce play a different role from question word gaps. Take the definite description 'the list' in 1.c. Here, Tim is talking about a list which he assumes Gareth to be already familiar with. Let's see how this expression introduces a gap.

First, note that the expression 'the list' is part of the instruction or suggestion 'Check the list'. For the addressee, such an instruction only makes sense if he knows which list is meant. In other words, the instruction 'Check the list' has two component parts:

- a gap __ which needs to be filled by a list from the context
- an instruction or suggestion to check the object the filler stands for

At first sight, there is a problem, since 1.a and 1.b make no mention of a list. Perhaps, the notion of a context as the shared information introduced during a conversation is too narrow. This context of the immediate dialogue, the *discourse context*, needs to be enriched with information that the interlocutors already shared before the current conversation got started. We will refer to this enriched context as the *common ground* of Gareth and Tim. The common ground includes

- the discourse context
- information Gareth and Tim came to share in previous conversations or other activities
- background knowledge which they are presumed to share, e.g. by both living and working in Slough, England

For instance, in a previous conversation Tim and Gareth's manager, Brent, might have told them:

(4) A list with all our products and prices is in the pricing folder of the shared drive.

The indefinite noun phrase 'a list with all our products and prices' provides the filler for the gap introduced by 'the list'. The interplay between indefinites and definites as providing fillers and invoking informational gaps has led to modifications and extensions of the view of a context as simply a set of possibilities. It is beyond the scope of this chapter to elaborate on the full technical details of such a revised view. Nevertheless, let us try to explain what such an extended notion of context looks like; here we base our explanation on the approach that has been worked out in detail in Piwek (1998) and Piwek and Krahmer (2000).

The idea is to think of contexts as structured representations of the world (or how it might be, could be, is imagined to be, etc). This is in contrast with the eliminative view of context change that we have already come across and which views a context as an amorphous set of possible worlds. Contexts as structured representations first and foremost need to have counterparts for the things we individuate in everyday life—chairs, tables, houses, people, etc. We use the term *witness* for such a representational counterpart. An indefinite noun phrase, such as 'a list with all our products and prices', is seen as introducing a witness, a sign or proof of something. The descriptive content of the noun phrase ('list' and 'with all our products and prices') is taken as contributing a classification of the object that the witness stands for. This is achieved through labels that attach to the witness in the structured representation, see Figure 9.2. This figure also visualises the import of the definite noun phrase 'the list', as a gap with a label that specifies the type of filler it requires.

Figure 9.2 is an example of a structured context that is inhabited by a witness (the small box in the context) and two labels that are attached to the witness. The witness, which has been introduced through the use of an indefinite noun phrase ('a . . . '), stands for an object in the world and the labels classify the object via the witness. This context provides a filler for

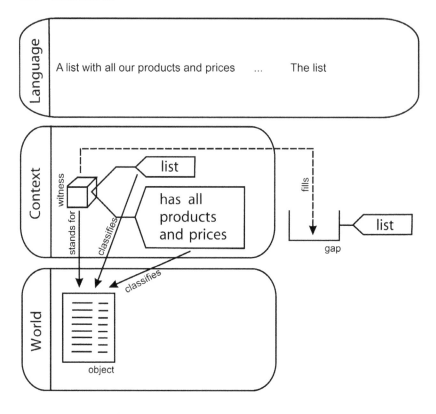

Figure 9.2 Example of a structured context that is inhabited by a witness and two labels attached to the witness.

a gap, introduced by a definite noun phrase ('the . . . '), that requires a witness that is labelled as being a list.

Thus, whereas indefinites introduce new witnesses, definites introduce gaps that require filling by witnesses that are already present in the context. The difference between the two types of expression is highlighted by their very different behaviour under negation:

(5) a. John buys a car.
    b. John buys the car.
(6) a. John didn't buy a car.
    b. John didn't buy the car.

When an indefinite is part of a negative sentence such as 6.a, the indefinite no longer introduces a witness: the sentence no longer commits the speaker to the existence of a car. In contrast, a definite, even when part of a negative sentence (6.b) still demands the existence of a car in the context. We can paraphrase 6.b as there is a car which John didn't buy. This property of definites, survival under negation, was first discussed by Gottlob Frege (one of the founders of Modern Symbolic Logic), who used the term presupposition ('Voraussetzung') for the type of information associated with definites.

So, we have now seen two different views of context: as a set of possible worlds and as a structured representation inhabited by witnesses and labels. We have seen that structured representations, in combination with the notion of an informational gap, provide a neat way to account for the effects of indefinite and definite noun phrases. Hans Kamp (1988) takes this one step further by arguing that the view of contexts as sets of possible worlds is incapable of dealing properly with the interaction of indefinites and pronouns. The example he uses to make this point is

(7) a. Exactly one of the ten balls is not in the bag.
   b. It is under the sofa.
(8) a. Exactly nine of the ten balls are in the bag.
   b. It is under the sofa.

Imagine that both 7.a and 8.a are uttered in a context in which the interlocutors do not share any information; in other words, everything is possible. So we start with the same context for both 7.a and 8.a. Both sentences lead to a new context in which there are ten balls of which nine are in the bag and one is not. In other words, both sentences result in the same set of possible worlds. But now suppose the speaker continues with 7.b or 8.b. For 7.b, 'It' picks up the ball that is not in the bag. In contrast, 'It' in 8.b can not be taken to refer to that ball. So it seems that the context for 'It' in 7.b is different from that in 8.b. But according to the possible worlds view of context change, there is no difference. In the words of Kamp (1988, p.158):

> We must conclude that no difference can be predicted if contexts are identified with sets of possible worlds. Therefore, a theory of meaning and context dependent interpretation of English must, if it is to handle such examples successfully, adopt a representation of contexts that goes beyond what sets of possible worlds are able to reveal.

COOPERATION: RULES AND RULE BREAKING IN DIALOGUE

Chess is primarily a competitive game. This can obscure the fact that playing chess requires a great deal of cooperation: both players need to obey the rules of chess and take turns in an orderly fashion, one after the other. Similarly, conversation, even though it can be adversarial, as in a dispute, requires the interlocutors to cooperate. Arguably, in conversation cooperation amounts to working towards the same end of effectively exchanging information.

Principle 3:   *Effective information flow is a cooperative endeavour.*

In the field of linguistics, the view of conversation as a cooperative endeavour has taken hold ever since the philosopher H. Paul Grice (1913–1988) delivered his influential William James lectures at Harvard University in 1967. The first part of these lectures was published as Grice (1975). In those lectures Grice proposed four specific rules that cooperative dialogue participants should adhere to and which, if followed, result in effective information flow. Here let us provide short paraphrases of these four rules:

QUANTITY:	Say no more and no less than is required.
QUALITY:	Be truthful
RELATION:	Be relevant.
MANNER:	Express yourself clearly. Be brief, orderly and avoid obscure or ambiguous expressions.

Of course, participants do not always follow these rules. First, they can explicitly opt out. A good example of a speaker opting out of QUANTITY can be found in an article that appeared in *The Times* on 27 June 2008, some months before the troubled bank HBOS was taken over by Lloyds TSB plc, which in turn had to be rescued by the UK Treasury:

> (9) Lord Stevenson of Coddenham [chairman of HBOS] told about 400 retail investors at HBOS's general meeting, in Edinburgh, that for legal reasons he could not state his true feelings about the hedge fund managers thought to have forced down HBOS's share price through short-selling on the back of false rumours. (Seib, 2008)

Violation can also be intentional and covert, for instance, when someone breaks the QUALITY rule by intentionally telling a falsehood. Unintentional violations will often have a comical effect. Take the utterance 1.b in example 1: Gareth's guess at the price of Opti-Bright Laser Copy Paper is a blatant violation of RELATION, following on Tim's utterance 1.a. The comical effect is enhanced further by Tim following up on Gareth's remark, without appearing to notice its irrelevance in the light of what he said in 1.a.

> (10) In this episode of the TV series *Father Ted*, the whistle of Benson, a groundskeeper, has gone missing.
> a. *BENSON:*   Anyway father, come on. Have you heard anything?
> b. *TED:*   About what?

c. *BENSON:*   About my whistle. [. . .] I've had that whistle for fifty years. It saved my grandfather's life.

d. *TED:*   Did it really?

e. *BENSON:*   Yes. He was being executed by the British. They had him up against the wall and they shot him. And the bullets all hit the whistle in his coat pocket and bounced off him.

f. *TED:*   Really? The bullets bounced off him.

g. *BENSON:*   Yes.

h. *TED:*   God almighty! So he survived?

i. *BENSON:*   No, no. They just reloaded and shot him again.

From 'The old grey whistle theft', episode 4 of the second series of the TV series *Father Ted* (Linehan and Mathews, 2000, p.145).

This example is a further illustration of an apparently unintentional violation, this time of QUANTITY. When Benson says that 'It [the whistle] saved my grandfather's life', his dialogue partner Ted assumes that Benson says no more and, importantly, no less than is required. If one says that 'X saved Y's life', the implicit assumption is that Y went on to live for a significant amount of time. This is, in particular, the case if one refers to this event in order to justify the importance of X for the speaker. In contrast, if a speaker uses the phrase 'X saved Y's life' and Y actually died shortly after the event, the speaker should provide this additional information. The information that Y died shortly after the event affects the evaluation of the importance of X to the speaker. Not providing the information that is required to correctly evaluate the justification violates the injunction to say no less than is required for the effective exchange of information. After all, with Benson's grandfather not surviving, the importance of the whistle is greatly diminished, only having bought Benson's grandfather a few extra moments.

A third type of violation Grice labels 'flouting'. In these cases, the speaker intentionally and publicly violates a rule. This violation usually serves a clear purpose: for instance, to communicate information which the speaker doesn't want to commit to explicitly. For these cases, it is essential that the addressee recognises that violation has occurred and can work out what the speaker really meant.

The report on HBOS Chairman Lord Stevenson's speech to HBOS's general meeting (see example 9) continues with Lord Stevenson referring to the hedge fund managers who were instrumental in forcing down HBOS's share price through short selling as:

(11)   "Very nice people", he said with a grimace. (Seib, 2008)

A blatant flouting of QUALITY (Be truthful). Grice explains instances of this kind as follows:

> It is perfectly obvious to A [the speaker] and his audience that what A has said or has made as if to say is something he does not believe, and the audience knows that A knows that this is obvious to the audience. So, unless A's utterance is entirely pointless, A must be trying to get across some other proposition than the one he purports to be putting forward. This must be some obviously related proposition; the most obviously related proposition is the contradictory of the one he purports to be putting forward. (1975, p.53)

In other words, sometimes speakers choose to break the rules of conversation to communicate with their audience in a way which allows them to convey something and yet be less committed than would be the case if they had said it explicitly.

CONCLUDING REMARKS

At the heart of this chapter is the analogy between conversations and games of correspondence chess. This analogy led us to three principles of information flow which can be summarised as the three Cs of information flow in a dialogue game: Context change, Context dependence and Cooperation. We examined the influential model of context change as elimination of possibilities, and then moved on to the role of informational gaps and context change. We identified a limitation of the view of contexts as sets of possible worlds and considered the alternative of contexts as structured representations. Finally, we turned to the insight that effective information exchange requires cooperation. We discussed Grice's four rules of cooperation in dialogue and examined the, at first sight, paradoxical fact that violating these rules can in itself be a form of cooperative information flow. At this point, we also seemed to have arrived at the limits of the analogy between correspondence chess and dialogue.

FURTHER READING

This chapter provides a rough outline of the mechanisms underlying information flow in dialogue. Wherever possible, I have included references to the detailed, often technical, studies that underpin this chapter. Even so, there are many issues and problems that were beyond the scope of this chapter. I conclude by highlighting a few of these.

When discussing context change, the concern has been primarily with the effect that statements have on the context. Conversations have an abundance of other types of utterances, including instructions, clarifications and questions. For example, Ginzburg (1996) argues that to deal with the effect of question–asking on the context, an even more elaborate structural account of context than the one discussed here is called for. Traum (1994) presents one of the first computational accounts of how interlocutors come to ground, i.e. agree on information that has been introduced in conversation (recall the simplifying assumption about grounding that we made in the second section of this chapter). Recently, there have been efforts to arrive at an International Organization for Standardization (ISO) standard for characterising the rich tapestry of dialogue acts that occur in dialogue (Bunt et al., 2010). Other issues that we have had to skim over include the interaction between verbal utterances and gesture in information exchange (e.g. Lascarides and Stone, 2009), intonation (see the collection of papers in Bosch and van der Sandt, 1999), vagueness (a complex topic which is dealt with in the accessible monograph of van Deemter, 2010) and ambiguity (specifically the nocuous variety that arises when addressees interpret the same utterance differently, see Willis et al., 2008).

ACKNOWLEDGEMENTS

I would like to thank Richard Power, Svetlana Stoyanchev and Sandra Williams for helpful feedback on a draft of this paper.

NOTES

1. Assuming arrival times are expressed in hours and minutes, prior to I's utterance of e, the arrival could be on each minute of the day, resulting in a context with at least as many alternatives/possible worlds as there are minutes in a day. This, of course, assumes that it is already part of the context that the flight arrives on the day of the conversation.
2. For example, if someone makes a claim but actually believes the opposite (in the vernacular, she or he is lying or perhaps just confused, depending on whether they intend to mislead the addressee), they will still incur a commitment. Hamblin has also pointed out that not only can people issue statements but also, for instance, institutions. Our common sense notion of belief, as the mental state of a person, fails to do justice to such cases, in contrast to a view of contexts as populated by commitments.

BIBLIOGRAPHY

Bosch, P. and van der Sandt, R. (1999) *Focus: Linguistic, Cognitive, and Computational Perspectives*, Cambridge, Cambridge University Press.

Bunt, H., Alexandersson, J., Carletta, J., Choe, J., Chengyu Fang, A., Hasida, K., Lee, K., Petukhova, V., Popescu-Belis, A., Romary, L., Soria, C. and Traum, D. (2010) 'Semantic Annotation Framework (SemAF), Part 2: Dialogue Acts', *ISO Draft International Standard ISO 24617–2*, May 2010.

Fillmore, C. (1981) 'Pragmatics and the Description of Discourse', in Cole, P. (ed.), *Radical Pragmatics*, New York, Academic Press, pp.143–166.

Gervais, R. and Merchant, S. (2002) *The Office: The Scripts: Series 1*, London, BBC Worldwide Limited.

Ginzburg, J. (1996) 'Dynamics and the Semantics of Dialogue', in Seligman, J. (ed.), *Language, Logic and Computation*, vol. 1, Stanford, CSLI.

Grice, H.P. (1975) 'Logic and Conversation', in Cole, P. and Morgan, J. (eds.), *Syntax and Semantics 3: Speech Acts*, New York, Academic Press, pp.41–58.

Hamblin, C. (1970) *Fallacies*, London, Methuen and Co. Ltd.

Kamp, H. (1988) 'Comments', in Grimm, R. and Merrill, D. (eds.), *Contents of Thought*, Tucson, University of Arizona Press, pp.156–181.

Lascarides, A. and Stone, M. (2009) 'A Formal Semantic Analysis of Gesture', *Journal of Semantics*, 26(4), pp.393–449.

Linehan, G. and Mathews, A. (2000) *Father Ted: The Complete Scripts*, London, Boxtree.

Piwek, P. (1998) *Logic, Information and Conversation*, unpublished PhD thesis, Eindhoven, Eindhoven University of Technology.

Piwek, P. and Krahmer, E. (2000) 'Presuppositions in Context: Constructing Bridges', in Bonzon, P., Cavalcanti, M. and Nossum, R. (eds.), *Formal Aspects of Context*, Dordrecht, Kluwer Academic Publishers.

Prüst, H., Minnen, G. and Beun, R.J. (1984) *Transcriptie dialoogexperiment juni/ juli 1984*, Eindhoven, IPO Rapport no. 481.

Seib, C. (2008) 'Regulators Are Failing to Crack Down on Financial Crimes, HBOS Chairman Says', *The Times*, 28 June, p.53.

Simon, H. (1996) *The Sciences of the Artificial*, Cambridge, Massachusetts, MIT Press.

Stalnaker, R. (1999) *Context and Content*, Oxford, Oxford University Press.

Traum, D. (1994) *A Computational Theory of Grounding in Natural Language Conversation*, PhD Thesis, New York, University of Rochester.

Turing, A. (1950) 'Computing Machinery and Intelligence', *Mind*, vol. 59, no. 236, pp.433–460.

Van Deemter, K. (2010) *Not Exactly: In Praise of Vagueness*, Oxford, Oxford University Press.

Willis, A., Chantree, F., and De Roeck, A. (2008) 'Automatic Identification of Nocuous Ambiguity', *Research on Language and Computation*, vol. 6, no. 3–4, pp.355–374.

WorldsBestChatbot.com (2009) '2009 Loebner Prize Competition Transcripts', http://www.worldsbestchatbot.com/Competition_Transcripts   (Accessed   1 August 2010).

10 Quantum Information

Tony Nixon

INTRODUCTION

My intention in this chapter is not to give a full and comprehensive description of quantum information but to try to give some insights into ways in
which thinking about information in the world of quantum physics is forced
to differ from the traditional classical perspective. When I refer to quantum
information as a field, I include general aspects such as quantum computing
and any system where the information is stored or transferred as quantum
states. I will briefly describe how measurements on quantum systems are
interpreted and give some idea of their consequences when applied to such
things as the construction of logic gates, encryption and computing.

WHY QUANTUM?

The word 'quantum' is often used to describe a discrete quantity or change.
In science, the word has a similar meaning because, when we observe the
physical world in detail, we find that everything seems to be constructed
from discrete packets. At first sight this might seem unremarkable; we're
all used to the idea of particles such as electrons, protons or neutrons,
which are discrete. So what's the fuss about? Well, to give a less obvious
example, light is composed of discrete packets of energy which we call
photons. These photons appear to move like any other particle (albeit
very quickly) taking straight lines between source and destination; however, on closer observation they appear to do some very odd things as
well. Force them through a narrow slit, and they emerge, not as a narrow
beam, but as a divergent spread. Force them through two narrow slits
placed close together, and the spread develops dark patches, like no-go
areas. Oddly, if the intensity of the light beam is reduced, it is possible
to observe the arrival of individual photons. Each photon's behaviour is
altered by the presence of the second slit despite the fact one could argue
that as a particle it must have passed through only one of the slits. What
often seems more surprising is that this odd behaviour isn't confined to

photons, it can be observed with things that are more obviously particulate, such as atoms or even quite large molecules (Arndt et al., 1999). In fact, it's not something peculiar about light that causes this behaviour, but rather something about the nature of physical laws, which is only observable under certain conditions. The laws that govern this behaviour are not like those we observe in the everyday world described by Isaac Newton over 300 years ago and usually referred to as *classical* mechanics. These are the laws of quantum mechanics constructed by the likes of Niels Bohr, Albert Einstein, Erwin Schrödinger and many others over the first half of the last century, and they offer an alternative description of information in the physical world. Unlike the other major departure from classical physics at the turn of the last century (relativity, which was largely the work of Einstein over ten years or so), quantum theory evolved slowly and was the work of many individuals. Quantum mechanics (which describes the way particles interact at the atomic scale, based on quantum theory) is a more fundamental description of the world than that given by classical mechanics, but, of course, at macroscopic scales the quantum and classical descriptions agree entirely.

Given that quantum theory has been with us for about a century, it has been surprisingly slow to have an impact on the way that we perceive, manipulate and store information. In fact, in computing and information technology (IT), where small scale devices are concerned, it is often considered to be a nuisance best avoided. That's not to say that these devices don't rely on quantum laws to work; the whole of solid-state electronics relies on quantum laws, but it does so by averaging the quantum effects and thus suppressing certain aspects of their quantum nature. Classical information—that is information that obeys classical laws—is fundamentally different from quantum information, and it is this perceived difference that I want to explore in this chapter.

It is well known that these quantum laws have never sat comfortably in the minds of many physicists. In 1982 the Nobel Laureate Richard Feynman said

> Might I say immediately, so that you know where I really intend to go, that we always have had (secret, secret, close the doors!) we always have had a great deal of difficulty in understanding the world view that quantum mechanics represents. (Feynman, 1982, p.471)

That's not to say that we don't know how to use them. Quantum theory makes predictions which have been verified experimentally to better than one part in 10^8 (Gabrielse et al., 2007) by comparing observed values of the fine structure constant with those predicted by theory, but we do have serious difficulty in rationalising them. In itself this is fascinating! We have a set of laws which we can apply with huge precision, and yet, as you will see, arguments have raged for nearly a century about their interpretation.

When we move to describing the world at an atomic scale, the impact of interacting with a particle, say, an electron or a proton, to make a measurement becomes very significant. In fact, it becomes *impossible* to make a measurement of one kind without losing information of another. Essentially, quantum theory places limits on what it is possible to observe; the more precisely we identify the position of a particle, the less we know about its momentum and vice versa. This is the basis of the famous Heisenberg uncertainty principle which puts a limit on how much we can know about a system. It is vital to understand that this loss of information in the measurement process is not something which can be overcome by using a better apparatus or improving the experiment; the loss of accuracy is a fundamental property of the physical world.

The consequence of there being a physical limit to our knowledge of a system raises important questions about how we describe the state of such systems. At the heart of our physical description of the world lies the notion of a state. The state is a complete mathematical description of a physical system. Thinking classically this might be the state of a light switch; we are all used to the notion that a light switch can be in one of two states, on or off. In quantum mechanics things are much less straightforward because the quantum switch can be simultaneously on and off. This property of the physical world seemed so paradoxical that Erwin Schrödinger constructed a thought experiment to show how unreasonable indeterminacy is if drawn into the macroscopic world of our everyday experience. The basic principle was simple: use an event which was subject to uncertainty to trigger an event in the macroscopic world which is hidden from the observer. Then ask how we should interpret that event whilst it remains unobserved. Incidentally, this is a thought experiment; so far as I know, no cats were ever harmed by Schrödinger!

Take one cat and isolate it in a lightproof, soundproof box. In the same box, place a capsule containing a poisonous gas, the release of which is triggered by a device which relies on a random quantum event, usually the radioactive decay of a particle. Seal the box and wait for a period of time such that there is a 50% probability that the poison has been released and then ask the question, what is the state of the cat? Quantum mechanics tells us that the cat is both dead and alive! Let me be absolutely clear about this, it is not that the cat has a chance of being *either* dead *or* alive or that it is in some way half dead. It is that it is simultaneously in both states: dead *and* alive. When the box is opened, the ambiguity vanishes as the state is determined by observation, and the cat is found to be in one of the two observable states *either* dead *or* alive. (In the language of quantum mechanics, we say that the state *collapses* when it is observed.) Schrödinger's aim in suggesting this experiment was to draw attention to the unreasonable worldview that quantum mechanics represents.

Usually thought experiments would be better defined than this and in practice there are various details which make it impractical to even consider as a serious experiment. But the point here is simply to draw attention to the nature of quantum information as opposed to classical information. In the quantum world a switch can be simultaneously 'on' and 'off', but only whilst it remains unobserved. We refer to this as a *superposition* of the states 'on' and 'off'. 'On' and 'off' are characteristic states of the system or, in the language of quantum mechanics *eigenstates*, 'eigen', from the German for 'innate'.

Schrödinger's cat also demonstrates the importance of the role of observation in quantum mechanics. There are many philosophical questions which arise around the issues of exactly what constitutes observation and where various boundaries lie. Observation of the state of a quantum system yields a result which is consistent with the cat being in an eigenstates i.e. *either* dead *or* alive. Exactly what constitutes observation is a really interesting question; speaking pragmatically, we can think in terms of how isolated the system is from its surroundings (this is an issue to which I will return). The more a system is coupled to its environment the less likely it is to exhibit quantum properties; in particular, superposition which is essential for the exploitation of quantum information. That is to say, information about the state of the system should not leak out in some way. This, from an engineering perspective, can be very difficult to achieve because a single photon entering or leaving the system could cause its state to collapse. This loss of isolation is referred to as decoherence. Terms like 'superposition' and 'decoherence' are properties more usually associated with waves, and, as you will see shortly, this is because waves are at the core of our thinking when working with quantum mechanics.

Any *observation* of Schrödinger's cat will yield the result dead *or* alive. In this case we have set up the experiment so that there is a 50% chance of observing the cat dead and 50% alive. Someone conducting the experiment, unaware that there is a 50/50 probability of finding the cat alive, could only derive these odds by repeating the experiment several times and watching the outcomes converge to give roughly equal numbers of each eigenstate. So, based on a single measurement, it is not possible to say anything about the probability distribution of states which contribute to the superposition. This is an important point. What takes place in the box is random and not accessible; any attempt to look will result in a collapse of the superposition.

At the heart of the quantum description sits the wave function, a mathematical function that describes the possible states of a system. The wave function is complex in the mathematical sense of being composed of real and imaginary parts, and it is not observable. The square of the wave function's modulus gives a function which is the amplitude of the probability for observing the system in one of its eigenstates. It is the wave function that produces many of the strange properties that we infer from observation of quantum systems. This is in no small part due to the fact that the wave function can be negative (which is not possible for a probability—remember that the probability for observing the system in a particular eigenstate relates to the *square* of the wave function), so when combined with another wave function that is positive, can sum to zero. So, for example, this may then yield a probability of zero for finding a particle in a particular place—hence my remark earlier about no-go areas when photons are forced through slits.

Returning to Schrödinger's cat, it is possible to identify various physical systems which have properties which are mutually exclusive such as the direction of spin of a particle. We could try to use these systems in the same way that we might use binary switches to convey information.

QUBITS

The key element of quantum information is the quantum bit. The equivalent of the bit used in classical information; the quantum bit (usually abbreviated to qubit or Qbit) embodies similar properties to the classical bit in that it can be observed to be either a 0 or a 1. However, when prepared appropriately and isolated, it can be described as being in a superposition of both 0 and 1. In this preparation we could also choose the proportion of the qubit that is 1 and the proportion that is 0. It is, to say the least, challenging to understand how the qubit being in a superposition of states can be of any value, let alone of greater value than a classical bit but this is a key part of what makes quantum information so different from its classical counterpart.

As a part of the answer to this paradox, consider a simple classical operation converting a bit from a 0 to a 1 or vice-versa. To achieve this, we would use a logic device called a NOT gate which outputs the opposite of its input. Working with classical information, this is the only possible nontrivial (it is possible to have a logic gate which does nothing) *reversible* operation which can be performed on a single bit. By reversible I mean that the original information is not lost when processed through a gate; if I know what was done, I can recover the original data. Take as a counter-example the operation ERASE, which converts every bit to 0; after carrying out this operation, there is no way of knowing which bits were 0 and which were 1. In the case of NOT, I can simply run the bits through another NOT gate to recover the original bit pattern and thus the operation NOT is reversible. When working with qubits the function of the equivalent to a NOT gate shifts the proportions of the superposition, so we replace a mixture of 0 and 1 with a mixture of 1 and 0. Only if the superposition were exactly half and half would the value of the qubit remain unchanged. Additionally, there are infinitely many single-bit reversible operations available using qubits, depending on the proportions of 0 and 1 that I choose, whereas there is only one operation (NOT) using classical bits.

There are many constraints on qubits which simply don't exist in the classical world; here are two examples. First, all quantum logic operations have to be reversible. Therefore many classical 2-bit gates are impossible.

For example, a 2-bit AND gate would be forbidden because 00, 01 and 10 all become 0 when ANDed, and it is not possible to recover the original data after the process has taken place. Second, it is not possible to make a copy of a qubit, which is referred to as the no-cloning theorem (Wootters and Zurek, 1982). One can prepare several qubits in the same state, but it is not possible to make a copy of a single qubit. Any attempt to copy a qubit would amount to observation of its state, and this would result in a collapse of the superposition. This presents an interesting restriction since it is not possible to use the output from a logic gate as an input to several other logic gates as is common practice in classical logic design (FANOUT as it is called). These along with various other restrictions make quantum information challenging to work with.

Two applications in the field of quantum information are potentially very rewarding, quantum encryption and quantum computing. Quantum computers still seem to be something for the more distant future; however, quantum encryption has been carried out over considerable distances and shows real promise.

ENTANGLEMENT AND QUANTUM ENCRYPTION

Quantum encryption is based on the Einstein–Podolsky–Rosen (EPR) paradox first published in 1935 (Einstein, Podolsky and Rosen, 1935). The paradox suggests that a pair of particles, prepared appropriately then separated by a vast distance, would be able to communicate instantaneously, thus violating *locality*, which limits communication speeds to being no faster than the speed of light. The paradox goes as follows: Alice[1] prepares a pair of qubits whose values are opposite. This is quite common in subatomic physics where decay processes take place which have to obey certain conservation laws. In this case the net spin of the two particles is zero. (In practice this is actually done using the polarisation of photons, but the principles are essentially the same.) These particles are said to be '*entangled*' since even when separated their respective spins should sum to zero. Having prepared the particles, she gives one of them to Bob who flies off to some remote location. Alice then measures the spin of her particle along an axis, let's call it the z-axis. She will obtain a result of either + or − since these are the two eigenstates for the measurement of a particle's spin. Bob then measures the spin of his particle along the same z-axis and obtains a result opposite to Alice. So if Alice measured + Bob obtains −, and the net result is zero. So far all is well. But suppose that Bob doesn't measure along the z-axis but uses the x-axis (at right angles to z) instead, the outcome of Bob's measurement will now be + or − with equal probability. This is because Heisenberg's uncertainty principle prohibits knowing simultaneously the angular momentum in both axes, and since Alice knows it in z, it cannot be determined in x, even for Bob's particle because that would determine it for Alice's particle too. So, if Bob measures in z, he always gets the same result, but in x he could get either result with equal probability (see Figure 10.1). In Figure 10.1, Alice entangles a pair of particles and gives one to Bob who flies away. Alice measures her particle, and this determines the state of Bob's. Bob will get a random result if he measures in x but always correlates with Alice if he measures in z.

Now this presents a problem. Since Alice made her measurement after the particles were separated, how and when was the information transferred to Bob's particle such that Bob sees differing results in x and z? At first sight it seems that information has passed between Alice and Bob, but this is not the case.

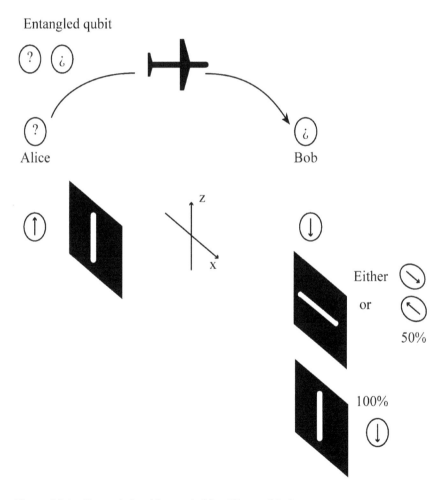

Figure 10.1   Entangled qubits carried by Alice and Bob.

The outcome of an individual measurement simply tells us what one of the eigenstates is, and Bob only has one chance at making the measurement. If he measures in the *z*-axis, he has no way of knowing that he has made a different measurement to Alice until he sees the result of Alice's measurement. As a result, despite appearances to the contrary, information isn't actually transferred until Bob compares results with Alice. Interestingly, entanglement does lead to some fascinating applications.

Currently the security of encryption systems, such as Rivest, Shamir and Adleman (RSA), relies upon the time required to make lengthy calculations. The sheer time taken to find factors of a very large number, for example, mean that for all practical purposes these systems are secure. However, quantum entanglement offers any desired level of security and further, it will detect any attempt at hacking. The technique is quite straightforward, once EPR is understood. Essentially the question is how does Alice pass to Bob a series of zeros and ones which form the key to an encrypted message? Alice can prepare a series of pairs of entangled qubits keeping one from each pair for herself and giving the other to Bob. She then makes a series of measurements of her entangled qubits and use the outcome of those measurements, say + + − + − − +, to produce a key. If Bob knows the correct axis to measure along, he can extract from Alice's key the exact reverse of Alice's key used to encrypt the message. Simply inverting this gives him the key.

You can see that there is a flaw in this process because Alice and Bob have to agree an axis to make their measurements and if they have to meet to do this, they might as well exchange keys. However, it is possible to determine a key without meeting. If Alice measures her qubits choosing *x*- and *z*-axes at random whilst Bob does the same, they both end up with a random series of + and −. Now it is possible for Alice and Bob to discuss in public the sequence of axes they each used: so Alice says something like 'I used: *z, x, x, z, x, z, z, z*' and Bob says 'I used: *z, z, x, z, x, x, z, x*' anyone watching (including Bob and Alice) can see that terms 1, 3, 4, 5 and 7 match.

Bob and Alice, and only Bob and Alice, know the values of the measurements for those qubits, and they have exchanged a key successfully.

Finally, what happens if a third party, Eve, is listening in? Eve might intercept the entangled qubits meant for Bob. She makes measurements on them, then passes them on to Bob and waits for their public exchange to take place. The problem for Eve is that the qubits she passes to Bob are

Table 10.1   Alice and Bob's Measurements

Alice	z	x	x	z	x	z	z	z
Bob	z	z	x	z	x	x	z	x
Match	yes	no	yes	yes	yes	no	yes	no

not in the same state, after she has performed her measurements, as they were before. Each time Eve makes a measurement, she has a 50% risk of altering the state of the qubit she measures. This means that Bob and Alice can exchange a brief message encrypted using a subset of the key to test for eavesdroppers. There are many approaches that Eve might take such as preparing the qubits then sending them to Alice and Bob; in all cases she will be detected.

In practice things are never quite so perfect. There is, in fact, no way of distinguishing between differences due to eavesdropping and those due to errors which occur because of noise (i.e. the qubits interacting with their environment). Error correction is challenging in quantum information because of the no-cloning theorem; however, it is not impossible. This is fortunate because otherwise noise would render nearly all information processing impossible.

QUANTUM COMPUTERS

The invention of a quantum computing as a field is generally attributed independently to Richard Feynman (1982) and to David Deutsch (1985). Essentially Feynman spotted the need and Deutsch developed a quantum version of the Turing machine—a fundamental first step in the field.

It is important to understand that quantum systems—qubits, quantum gates, quantum computers—are *fundamentally* different from classical systems. In the 1960s, fluidics, the study of the motion and switching of fluids, was under close scrutiny as a technology for producing fast calculators and computers. These systems were, for a time, in competition with electronic systems based on transistors. The principles that they used for computing were no different to the electronic systems, both functioned classically. Their forms were entirely different, but their function was identical; they obeyed the laws of classical physics. Quantum systems obey the laws of quantum physics. This implies that in order to work with quantum information we have to use components that obey quantum laws. So what are the options and to what uses might they be put?

The principles of how to construct quantum computers using quantum logic gates and circuits are well understood, and there are many properties of physical systems that fulfil the requirements for quantum information processing and storage: excited states in atoms, the polarisation of photons, the spin of electrons or nuclei and so on. Many different quantum devices have been demonstrated in the laboratory: however, these are very difficult to scale. The problem of decoherence (the loss of quantum behaviour because of potential observability) in systems that handle more than a small number of qubits, scale very quickly; and being able to hold several qubits in a state where they can be entangled with each other yet sufficiently isolated to prevent decoherence proves very difficult indeed. Amongst the technologies proposed for doing this are trapped ions, trapped neutral atoms, SQUIDs (superconducting quantum interference devices) and quantum dots. Historically, NMR (nuclear magnetic resonance) has proven to be most effective but recently seems to be in some decline. Interestingly, the classical computer industry is beginning to approach dimensions at which their components will start to exhibit quantum behaviour. As I said earlier this is currently viewed as a nuisance, but it may well provide another avenue of development.

So, assuming that it is possible to build such a device, what might it do? As you can see, working with quantum information is not easy; it is not intuitive and requires a quite deep understanding of physics and mathematics. To date, only a handful of algorithms have appeared for quantum computing. There seem to be three broad classes in which quantum algorithms outperform their classical counterparts, first, there are those based on Fourier transforms, such as Shor's algorithm (Shor, 1994) for integer factorisation, of which I will say more in a moment. Then there are quantum search algorithms the basic principles of which were discovered by Lov Grover (Grover, 1996), and finally there are quantum simulations. This last group of applications were in a sense the trigger for studying quantum information in the first place as outlined by Feynman in 1982 (Feynman, 1982). The number of quantum numbers required to simulate a quantum system grows exponentially with the size of the system. So if there are n components in the system of interest, then the description requires c^n bits of classical memory, where c is a constant determined by the details of the system. By contrast a quantum computer can perform such calculations using only kn qubits, where, again, k is a constant determined by the system. Even the most simple chemical structures are nearly impossible to simulate on a classical computer, whereas quantum computers could potentially one day open the door to simulating systems as complex as biological molecules. However, the reduction in resources seems to come at a price, as it is not clear how information relating to the wave function can be recovered from such simulations.

Probably the most famous quantum computing algorithm is Shor's algorithm for finding the prime factors of an integer, published in 1994. This is a particularly important discovery because, as I mentioned earlier, many encryption schemes (including RSA—one of the most popular) are based on the difficulty associated with finding factors of very large numbers. Typical classical computations for unravelling RSA encryption could take longer than the life of the universe, but on an appropriate quantum computer could be carried out in fractions of a second. As I have already described, quantum information has opened up new possibilities for encryption, and work in this field appears to be progressing quite quickly. On the other hand, at the time of writing, quantum computers capable of carrying out anything as complex as cracking RSA encryption still seem to be only a very distant possibility.

INTERPRETATIONS OF QUANTUM INFORMATION

The difficulties in arriving at any real-world interpretation of quantum mechanics has generated disputes spanning several generations, starting with Bohr and Einstein in the 1920s and 1930s. (In fact, even the history itself is a part of the dispute; with hindsight the positions of various protagonists seems far from clear.) The divide was centred around what later became known as the Copenhagen interpretation, which centred on Bohr's belief in what he called complementarity based on a paper that he gave at the 1927 Solvey (Whitaker, 2006) conference. 'Complementarity' referred to the general notion that an object can have attributes which appear to be mutually exclusive.

The idea is illustrated by the famous image of a vase and two faces (Figure 10.2); the image represents both things, but the observer's mind flicks between one and the other, observing the vase excludes seeing the faces. In his 1927 paper, Bohr applied complementarity specifically to quantum theory in respect of wave particle duality. Einstein, Schrödinger and others were opposed to Bohr's belief and felt that there should be an explanation

Figure 10.2   Complementarity, illustrated by the illusion of the vase or two faces.

which allowed for determinism. For example that, in some way, particles should have a definite position and momentum despite it being impossible to observe both.

During this period Einstein devised many thought experiments to refute Bohr's claims, but in every case Bohr was able to overcome Einstein's objections. In 1935 Einstein abandoned the approach of using thought experiments to identify flaws in Bohr's interpretation; however, he never relinquished his opinion that the universe existed independently of observation. One interesting aspect of the thought experiments, which was recognised by Bohr and many others, was that the boundary between the measuring device and the measured system (referred to as the Heisenberg cut) could not be defined uniquely. In extreme interpretations, certainly the measuring apparatus, and maybe even the brain of the observer, should be considered a part of the measured system, making the whole process highly subjective.

The quest to prove that particles should have a definite position and momentum became known as the search for hidden variables. Such was the influence of Bohr, that the Copenhagen interpretation dominated thinking from 1935 to well beyond his death in 1962 and, although alternative hidden variable interpretations were proposed by de Broglie, Everett, Bohm and later Bell (Whitaker, 2006; Everett, 1957), they were never given proper consideration. (Interestingly Everett's work formed the foundation of the currently popular many worlds [or multiverse] interpretation in which the real world splits to evolve down every possible path at each decision point.) This lack of consideration was in no small part due to von Neumann (von Neumann, 1955), who in 1932 had produced a proof that hidden variable explanations were not possible, however, in the mid-1960s John Bell (Bell, 1966) showed this proof to be based on a false assumption. Bell's work inspired many experiments which test reality and locality. These endeavours fall under the collective title of experimental philosophy, which tests the nature of quantum information at the most fundamental level seeking to answer deep questions about the nature of the reality and our role in understanding it.

SUMMARY

From a purely pragmatic viewpoint, quantum theory is astonishing in predicting experimental results and enabling us to understand and engineer objects at an atomic scale. I hope that I have succeeded in conveying how remarkable some of these applications are, both in their usefulness and in their value as a probe of our understanding of reality. Applications exploiting counter-intuitive aspects of quantum theory such as entanglement may well soon become a part of our everyday understanding of the world, and, if so, one wonders how they will impact on our understanding of the fundamental nature of information.

NOTES

1. I follow here the convention used in explanations of cryptography that names two communicating parties Alice and Bob, and a third party, attempting to eavesdrop, Eve.

BIBLIOGRAPHY

Arndt, M., Nairz, O., Vos-Andreae, J., Keller, C., Van Der Zouw, G. and Zeilinger, A. (1999) 'Wave–Particle Duality of C60 Molecules', *Nature*, vol. 401, no. 6754, pp.680–682.

Bell, J.S. (1966) 'On the Problem of Hidden Variables in Quantum Mechanics', *Reviews of Modern Physics,* vol. 38, no. 3, pp.447–452.

Deutsch, D. (1985) 'Quantum Theory, the Church-Turing Principle and the Universal Quantum Computer', *Proceedings of the Royal Society of London. A. Mathematical and Physical Sciences*, vol. 400, no. 1818, pp.97–117.

Einstein, A., Podolsky, B. and Rosen, N. (1935) 'Can Quantum-Mechanical Description of Physical Reality Be Considered Complete?', *Physical Review*, vol. 47, no. 10, pp.777–780.

Everett, H. (1957) '"Relative State" Formulation of Quantum Mechanics', *Reviews of Modern Physics,* vol. 29, no. 3, pp.454–462.

Feynman, R.P. (1982) 'Simulating Physics with Computers', *International Journal of Theoretical Physics*, vol. 21, no. 6/7, pp.467–488.

Gabrielse G., Hanneke, D., Kinoshita, T., Nio, M. and Odom, B. (2007) 'Erratum: New Determination of the Fine Structure Constant from the Electron g Value and QED', *Physical Review Letters*, vol. 99, no. 3, 039902.

Grover, L.K., (1996) 'A Fast Quantum Mechanical Algorithm for Database Search', *Proceedings of the 28th Annual ACM Symposium on Theory of Computing*, Philadelphia, 22–24 May 1996, New York, ACM, pp.212–219.

Shor, P. (1994) 'Algorithms for Quantum Computation: Discrete Logarithms and Factoring', *Proceedings of the 35th Annual Symposium on Foundations of Computer Science*, Santa Fe, 20–22 November 1994, Los Alamitos, California, IEEE Computer Society, pp.124–134.

von Neumann, J. (1955) *Mathematical Foundations of Quantum Mechanics,* translated from German by R.T. Beyer, Princeton, New Jersey, Princeton University Press.

Whitaker, A., (2006) *Einstein, Bohr and the Quantum Dilemma: From Quantum Theory to Quantum Information*, Cambridge, Cambridge University Press.

Wootters, W.K. and Zurek, W.H. (1982) 'A Single Quantum Cannot Be Cloned', *Nature,* vol. 299, no. 5886, pp.802–803.

11 Information Policy Making

Developing the Rules of the Road for the Information Society (or the Anatomy of a Digital Economy Act)

Ray Corrigan

INTRODUCTION

The boundaries of the world have changed. Now someone with a computer connected to the Internet has direct access, from the comfort of their home or office, to a printing press, communications most of us would not have dreamed of twenty-five years ago, and a world of entertainment, commerce and education.

In such an information society, the default rules of the road[1] are our information laws and, if Lawrence Lessig (1999) is to be believed, the architectures of our digital information systems. These laws govern such diverse areas as intellectual property, telecommunications, media and broadcasting, commerce, surveillance, intelligence and security, data management (data protection, retention and privacy), defamation, freedom of expression, network architectures and governance. They are nominally designed to control and regulate the flow of information.

Information law has traditionally resided in places far removed from the cognitive radars of all but the specialist lawyers, lobbyists and traditional industries built upon it. Yet this industrial-scale information regulation now applies at the level of the individual with an Internet-connected computer and so should be of concern to all of us.

I use the qualification 'nominally designed to control' information flows, above, in relation to information laws because it is not always clear that the policymakers fully understand the complexity or technology of the systems they are attempting to regulate or the actual effect their regulations will have in practice. I understand that this is a serious claim to make, but it is more a criticism of the policy-making process than of individual policymakers themselves or even the experts who advise them. It is also partly a function of Deborah Lipstadt's view that "reasoned dialogue has a limited ability to withstand an assault by the mythic power of falsehood" (1994, p.25).

In a short chapter such as this, it is difficult to do more than to outline such a theory and illustrate it with a case study and/or a few examples. I will do this by covering, in particular, the process which led to the passing of the Digital Economy Act (DEA) in the UK and the lessons we can learn from it. I have chosen the DEA only because it is a contemporary example of the kind of process that leads to such laws, not necessarily because it was especially unique. If anything, it constitutes a fairly typical illustration of this kind of process, particularly in relation to intellectual property and telecoms laws, as many scholars (e.g. Lessig, 1999; Marsden, 2010) have noted.

It has been argued, most eloquently by James Boyle (2008), that as a result of developments in technology and information policy, and more specifically intellectual property policy, we are facing a second enclosure movement. This time, however, rather than an enclosure of the grassy commons of eighteenth-century England, it is an enclosure of the commons of the mind. The DEA, in addition to being a nice example of information policy making in action, is another addition to Boyle's mind enclosure fences.

PRE-HISTORY

Gowers

Often the processes leading to information laws have long and tortuous histories. Whichever starting point gets picked will be open to criticism. The main story begins when a senior member of the United Kingdom (UK) government went on holiday in 2009, but before we get to that, I need to sketch out some pre-history, relating to two government reports that were supposed to lay the foundations for laws like the DEA.

Intellectual property law has been in a permanent state of flux since the World Wide Web hit public consciousness in the mid-1990s. By 2005 the UK government asked former editor of the Financial Times, Andrew Gowers, to review the UK intellectual property framework. Gowers published his review in December 2006 (Gowers, 2006). The review made a number of recommendations, the key guiding principles of which were

- Better enforcement against commercial scale intellectual property crime
- Reduced complexity of the intellectual property system
- Reformed copyright law to improve consumers rights e.g. to allow individuals to copy CDs onto MP3 players[2]
- No extension of copyright terms. (The music labels were particularly unhappy with this but lobbied successfully to have it circumvented at EU level)[3].

Recommendation 39 of the Gowers report suggested Internet service providers (ISPs) and the entertainment industry should agree on a set of protocols for dealing with individuals "engaged in 'piracy'". If they could not come to a satisfactory working relationship on this by 2007, then the government should consider legislating.

The story, from there, gets murky. It can be summed up by saying the ISPs and music companies did not see eye to eye on how illegal file sharing should be tackled, and the UK government didn't get round to legislating between 2007 and 2009.

THREE STRIKES, FRANCE AND THE EUROPEAN UNION (EU)

By 2007, however, the recording industry had managed to get a '3 strikes' (or 'graduated response') idea on the legislative agenda in France (Knights, 2007). The notion was that suspected illicit file sharers would get two warnings from their ISP, and on a third suspected offence, they would have their Internet connection cut off. This 'HADOPI'[4] (Haute Autorité pour la diffusion des oeuvres et la protection des droits sur Internet) law was passed, struck down by the courts, amended, passed again and eventually approved by the French Constitutional Council (Conseil Constitutionnel) in the autumn of 2009[5].

Whilst this was going on in France, the three strikes proposals also began to bounce around the institutions of the European Union. There have been a bucket load of intellectual property directives passed by the EU since the early 1990s in an effort to keep up with rapidly changing digital technologies. A key battle on copyright and three strikes played out in the context of the Telecoms Reform framework[6] negotiations between the EU parliament, the Commission and the Council of Ministers during 2008 and 2009.

The Commission and the Council of Ministers were largely in favour[7] of including copyright protection measures in the framework and the EU parliament were largely against this idea. The Parliament introduced an amendment to the framework which would have made it very difficult for EU member states to implement three strikes laws. This amendment was variously opposed and removed repeatedly by the Council, accidentally omitted by EU officials from official drafts of the directive and re-introduced repeatedly by the Parliament[8]. Eventually they compromised in November 2009, when the Parliament got to include wording which effectively meant "internet users should not get cut off . . ." and the Council and Commission got to add a qualifier meaning " . . . unless there is a good excuse"[9].

THE DIGITAL BRITAIN REPORT

I mention the French and EU background to illustrate that the UK is not operating in isolation with respect to copyright or other intellectual property and information laws. By 2009 the UK government still had not produced legislation to deal with illicit file sharing. The minister for communications, technology and broadcasting, Lord Carter, however, did publish the Digital Britain report in June 2009 (Carter, 2009). This was the government's policy blueprint to "secure the UK's position as one of the world's leading digital knowledge economies" (Carter, 2009, p.7).

The Digital Britain report included some legislative proposals to tackle file sharing (Carter, 2009, pp.111–113). Ofcom[10] would have a duty to instruct ISPs to send out warning letters to suspected infringers and collect data on those who got repeated warnings. With an appropriate court order, that data could be made available to rights holders to enable them to pursue civil court action against the suspects.

Ofcom would also get the power to require ISPs to throttle connections (e.g. through bandwidth reduction or protocol blocking) of suspected copyright infringers. This power would be triggered if the notification process had not reduced infringement by 70% within a year. It appears as though the throttling could be done without a court order, but the report does not mention disconnection as a possible sanction. Lord Carter was opposed to a disconnection option since it directly conflicted with one of the other aims of the report, to facilitate universal access to high-speed broadband.

The copyright provisions in the Digital Britain report were criticised by civil rights groups and ISPs as being too draconian and costly. Entertainment industry representatives expressed concern the measures did not go far enough to tackle online 'piracy'.

Lord Carter resigned from government immediately following the publication of the report.

THE DEA: THE ANATOMY OF AN ACT

The Gowers review, the Digital Britain report and the background from France and Brussels set the context for what came next in the UK.

The Making of the Act

In August 2009, Lord Peter Mandelson, the UK Secretary of State for Business, Innovation and Skills and President of the Board of Trade, went to Corfu on holiday, as a guest at the Rothschild family estate. Whilst he was there, he met philanthropist and entertainment mogul, David Geffen, founder of companies like Asylum Records and Dreamworks. The business secretary then returned from holiday, infused with an enthusiasm, which some argued was not previously in evidence, for clamping down on illicit file sharing on the Internet (Oliver, 2009).

Lord Mandelson is on record as saying:

> What I know about government is that if you think something is really important, you really have to get behind it . . . you have to have people following it through, forcing through the pace of change and new policy. (quoted by Wintour, 2010)

That's precisely what he did with the Digital Economy Bill, getting officials to rapidly draft legislation which was on the parliamentary agenda by November 2009.

The Gowers review had constituted the UK government's position on updating intellectual property laws until they changed their mind about copyright term extensions, which the report had categorically ruled out. Andrew Gowers himself was scathing about the government U-turn on this and about star-struck ministers enjoying photo opportunities with celebrities (Gowers, 2008).

Chapter 4 of the Digital Britain report, which stopped short of requiring disconnection of suspected illicit file sharers, formed the government's position (minus Lord Carter) from June until August 2009.

Immediately following the publication of the final Digital Britain report, the UK Department for Business Innovation and Skills (BIS) had launched a consultation on tackling illicit file sharing (BIS, 2009). The consultation contained at least one significant and potentially misleading error. The EU parliament amendment banning three strikes laws was still in the Telecoms Reform package at that time. The UK consultation misrepresented the wording of that amendment (BIS, 2009, p.13, S3.20). As phrased in the consultation, the EU amendment would *not* prevent EU member states introducing three strikes laws[11].

This error proved to be a minor story in the end, since the EU wording was eventually changed in a way that would allow three strikes, but the spectrum of mindsets of officials within government and which stakeholders in the drama capture their attention (e.g. creators, industry and/or individual citizens/consumers) is an important part of the process from which information laws emerge.

From August 2009, however, it seems to have been Lord Mandelson's belief in the importance of protecting the recording industry from mass copyright infringement on the Internet that energised the government into producing the Digital Economy Bill (Mandelson, 2009).

The Bill proved to be controversial.

Lord Mandelson made it clear that it would involve a three strikes regime to be implemented by 2011, but he had "no expectation of mass suspensions" of people's Internet services (BBC News, 2009). In addition there was a so-called 'Henry VIII' clause[12] in the Bill. This would enable the responsible Secretary of State (then Lord Mandelson) to change the Copyright, Design and Patents Act 1988 (CDPA) without having to go through Parliament. The idea was that the law could then be changed quickly to keep up with rapidly changing technology.

The measures attracted support from the recording and movie industries and popular singers like Lily Allen. They were opposed by consumer and civil rights groups, libraries and museums, ISPs, technology companies, some popular singers and songwriters (Topping, 2009) and the UK parliament's Joint Committee on Human Rights (2010)[13]. They also attracted a lot of lobbying on all sides, as acknowledged in the debate on the Bill in the House of Lords (Johnson, 2010; Cellan-Jones, 2010).

It is for the reader to judge the efficacy of the lobbyists' efforts in the state of the final wording of the Act. It is also possible to trace the evolution of the Bill through the Hansard report of proceedings in Parliament.[14]

I will look briefly here at the fate of Lord Mandelson's 'Henry VIII clause', however, clause 17 of the Bill. The idea that the incumbent Secretary of State in the relevant department should have the power to change copyright law without the interference of Parliament was strongly supported by the recording industry but widely criticised by, amongst others, the two main opposition parties, the Conservatives and the Liberal Democrats, and by the House of Lords Select Committee on Delegated Powers and Regulatory Reform. In the face of that criticism, the House of Lords decided to remove the controversial clause from the legislation in March 2010.

Amendment 120A was introduced by Lord Clement-Jones (a member of the Liberal Democrats' front bench) and Lord Howard (a Conservative and shadow minister for culture) and agreed by the House on 3 March 2010. In addition to removing clause 17, though, the amendment inserted another controversial provision that would facilitate Internet censorship at the request of copyright owners. Theoretically, a court order would be required to order an ISP "to prevent access to online locations". But ISPs would be liable for all legal costs involved "unless there were exceptional circumstances justifying the service provider's failure to prevent access despite notification by the copyright owner". Copyright owners were not under a similar obligation to pay ISPs' legal costs if their application for blocking was found to be unjustified. Given the asynchronous nature of the legal risks involved in this, it would most likely lead to a notice and block scheme in which ISPs would routinely filter, to the limits of the available technology[15], online locations flagged by copyright owners[16].

Shortly after the amendment was passed by the House of Lords, it became clear that it had been largely drafted by the British Phonographic Industry (BPI), the representative trade organisation of the UK recording industry. The Open Rights Group got access to the BPI's draft and made it available on their website. Amendment 120A was almost identical to the BPI draft, though in the House of Lords version there was extra consideration given to questions of national security, human rights and "the extent to which the copyright owner has made reasonable efforts to facilitate legal access to content". The BPI explained they had sent their proposed draft to the government and the opposition parties and that

> We made a proposal on this—and as is quite common—used statutory language to convey our point. (Arthur, 2010)

It is clear from this statement that the BPI regularly suggests draft intellectual property legislation to the UK government. This is common practice around the world for entertainment industry trade bodies. According to several scholars (Boyle, 1996; Litman, 2001; Lessig, 2001; Drahos with Braithwaite, 2002), they have been very successful at getting this draft legislation written into law.

It should be said that neither Lord Clement-Jones nor Lord Howard have any formal connection with the BPI, though the former is a partner at DLA Piper UK LLP, an international law firm[17] which has a significant intellectual property practice.

Nevertheless, Lord Whitty (Labour) was prompted by the process surrounding the development of the Bill to say

> I regret to say that during the course of our consideration of the Bill, we have seen one of the worst examples in my memory of the political parties being captured by a producer interest. That applies not only to the Government and the bringing forward of the Bill, but to the opposition Front Benches as well.[18]

Lord Whitty is the Chair of Consumer Focus, one of the consumer groups opposed to the Bill.

Less than a fortnight after it was passed in the House of Lords, amendment 120A also led to a revolt amongst the members of the Liberal Democrats at the party's spring conference. With their focus on the imminent general election and having apparently killed off Lord Mandelson's Henry VIII clause, the party leadership were expecting to be congratulated. They were completely blindsided by the vociferous opposition to their amendment. The conference passed an emergency motion condemning amendment 120A and the Digital Economy Bill generally "for focusing on illegal file-sharing rather than on nurturing creativity"[19].

Lord Clement-Jones reacted quickly to the criticism. He took advice from academics (Edwards, 2010a) and two days later in the third reading of the Bill in the House of Lords proposed amendments to the Internet censorship clause. These included an attempt to delete the presumption that ISPs would be responsible for legal costs involved if they failed to prevent access to an online location to the satisfaction of a copyright owner.

At this stage of proceedings, a general election was looming, and the Labour government planned to rush the Bill through the House of Commons in the 'wash-up' period. There is usually an interval between the Prime Minister announcing the date of a general election and the dissolution of Parliament. During this 'wash-up' period, the government cooperates with the opposition to rubber stamp legislation that is proceeding through Parliament without any further detailed scrutiny. It is traditionally only used with uncontentious bills.

The general election was shaping up to be the closest in modern times, and it is likely that the main parties were concerned to avoid the possibility of public criticism from pop stars during the campaign. Unsurprisingly, therefore, the Conservatives planned to support the 'wash-up' short circuiting of Parliament on the Digital Economy Bill (Wray, 2010).

Two campaign groups, the Open Rights Group and 38 Degrees then began a campaign to encourage members of the public to write to their members of Parliament objecting to it. Although more than 20,000 people did so (Barnett, 2010), the Bill passed into law on 7 April, 2010.

LAWMAKING IN TECHNICOLOR: WATCHING THEM REGULATING US

The public campaign against the Bill had encouraged significant numbers of people, for the first time, to tune into live debates in the House of Commons via the BBC Parliament channel, the BBC iPlayer and Twitter commentary. This piece of obscure information legislation in the UK was actually the biggest trending topic on Twitter worldwide for some days—involving about 25,000 Twitter messages from over 7000 people[20].

What they saw on 6 and 7 April was about seven hours of discussion taking place in a largely empty House of Commons chamber. On the final day the government introduced some amendments which were passed and Labour member of Parliament (MP) Tom Watson, who opposed the Bill, attempted to introduce some amendments that failed to go through[21]. At the end of the debate, the 'division' bell rang, and hundreds of MPs showed up and voted mostly in accordance with instructions from their party leadership. Most of the Labour attendees voted in favour. Most Conservatives did not take part in the vote at all. Well over half of all MPs, in fact, did not turn up for the vote. All of the Liberal Democrats who attended the final vote (about a third of all their MPs) opposed the Bill[22].

The MPs were aware the Bill was controversial. They had had an unprecedented number of e-mails from members of the public about it. Austin Mitchell even complained

> I have had lots of representations—mainly by e-mail, it has to be said, which is a nuisance; I find it difficult to deal with.[23]

But Mr Mitchell was one of the very few MPs to actually attend and actively take part in the shortened debate on those final two days. He spoke eloquently about the need for the House of Commons to be better informed.

> It is rather sad that we should devote one of the last major debates of this Parliament to such a sprawling rag-bag of a Bill . . . It is therefore difficult to come to any conclusion other than . . . that we should delay consideration until a better time when we can give the Bill more serious concern and preoccupation . . . this should not be a rushed Bill, carried on the basis of the half attention of a discredited, dying and distracted

Parliament. If the Bill is passed in that form, it will not have legitimacy and consent.[24]

Most MPs, unlike Mr Mitchell, simply failed to show up.

On the plus side, however, given the numbers of ordinary people who campaigned and watched, it was a great example of transparency in action—the law-making process exposed to the public gaze to a, perhaps, unprecedented degree. We need to be careful about how we interpret what we saw (Gyford, 2010)—MPs who were not in the chamber for the debate may also have been watching it on television (TV) or multi-tasking with other commitments while waiting to vote—but it is also an indication that transparency alone will not cure the problems in the political system (Marsden, 2010).

THE STAKEHOLDERS, THE DEA AND COMPETING STORIES

Broadly speaking in the intellectual property game, there are three generic sets of stakeholders:

- Creators
- Economic agents (businesses)
  - Content industry (publishing, recorded music, movies etc.)
  - Intermediaries (ISPs, search engines, libraries, collecting societies etc)
  - Technology companies
  - Others
- Consumers/citizens

For intellectual property or copyright to be effective, the needs of all of these stakeholders must be balanced. Theoretically, and if we had sufficient empirical evidence, we could build an economic model to work out where that balance should be struck (Corrigan and Rogers, 2005; Corrigan, 2008b). Unfortunately, there is very little empirical evidence available (Boyle, 2008).

Intellectual property laws tend to get passed on the basis of competing narratives rather than evidence, and the entertainment industries are exceptionally skilled at telling stories. A typical story in making the case for the DEA would run something like this:

Thousands of struggling young artists are having their work stolen by the hordes of the mass unwashed on the Internet. How are these poor young creators ever going to be able to survive or make a living from their work? The DEA will fix it.

It is persuasive. The protagonist—the young, invariably attractive, creative genius is suffering. The audience—the lawmakers in this case—empathise with this suffering and the emotional payoff is that they can alleviate the suffering. They can rescue the protagonist and indeed simultaneously save the 'creative industries', which reportedly lose hundreds of millions or even billions of pounds in the UK every year, by passing the DEA (Goldacre, 2009; GAO, 2010). Helping the little guy plays well to politicians. And in this case they get to help two of the main stakeholders, the creators and the economic agents. Well, some of the economic agents—the ISPs and technology giants are opposed, but that is fine too because the politicians are helping the little guy again, since economically speaking the recording industry is tiny compared with consumer electronics and technology markets. The emotional payoff is in helping the underdog and the practical payoff is in the belief it will generate good press and the photo opportunity with a celebrity.

The opposing story is more abstract:

> The protagonist is the citizen/consumer. Their Internet connections might be cut off, Web sites blocked, privacy invaded and freedom of expression curtailed, if the DEA gets passed.

In order for the audience to empathise, it helps if something bad happens to the protagonist at the start of the story. Nothing bad happens at the beginning—opponents are warning about what might happen. The structural legal dynamics are difficult to get a handle on—privacy and freedom of expression are nebulous concepts with fuzzy long term effects. The emotional pay off is fear (e.g. people will get excluded from the Net) and anger (e.g. 'the entertainment corporations are undermining our freedoms to protect outdated business models'). Academics and geeks understand the legal implications and deep technological, social and economic issues, but politicians like simple stories with simple fixes that can be quickly fed to the modern twenty-four hour news cycle. Fear stories on intellectual property play well to audiences of geeks but not to lawmakers, where they have to compete with things like terrorism, crime and immigration.

In addition geeks or academics are not stereotypically considered attractive or good communicators. Yet they have to be able to explain why their abstract and complicated story is important before their audience wanders off. Or alternatively the audience confuses the protagonist with the storyteller geek.

THE IMPLICATIONS OF THE DEA

The DEA covers a range of areas, including television and radio services, the electromagnetic spectrum, video games classification, public lending of electronic publications and others. Here I have mainly focussed on the evolution of the online copyright infringement provisions in the Act.

What does the Act, at the time of writing, have to say about copyright infringement?

In spite of all the amendments in the House of Lords, it has a number of Henry VIII clauses giving the Secretary of State the power to make regulations about how the law should work. This includes section 17, the "power to make provision about injunctions preventing access to locations on the internet". It does not seem entirely logical that a law should be passed and the detail worked out later, but the Secretary of State gets to decide how the Internet censorship should work. This section of the Act, however, does specify a number of restrictions on the conditions under which the relevant member of the government can take these decisions.

Only the development of detailed regulations by the Secretary of State and real test cases in the courts are going clarify the eventual boundaries of section 17 on Internet censorship. But at the time of writing, the position of search engines, businesses like airports and restaurants which provide free public Wi-Fi and possibly libraries and universities, is unclear, given the specific wording of section 17(4)(c) of the Act. A court will be able to issue a blocking injunction against "a location which has been, is being or is likely to be used to facilitate access to" other locations that are 'likely' be hosting infringing material. In the case of airports and restaurants, I would interpret 'location' in the sense of a physical rather than an online location.[25] How, for example, does the "internet of things" (Van Kranenburg, 2008) fit into this?

Does the Act include three strikes provisions?

Under section 9 the Secretary of State has the power to direct Ofcom to look into the need for 'technical measures' and figure out a code on how it should work in practice. Under section 10 the Secretary of State gets the power to order ISPs to implement 'technical measures' e.g. limiting the speed, limiting access to certain services or suspending a subscriber account. Again there are various conditions attached to how and when the Secretary of State imposes these technical measures.

So the Act does not include a detailed blueprint for a specific three strikes regime but gives the Secretary of State the power to implement such a scheme.

The potential legal problems with such a regime have been widely aired, most notably by Professor Lilian Edwards of Sheffield University School of law in the UK (Edwards, 2010b). A number of European high courts have also made rulings which indicate concerns about the boundaries of these kinds of information laws and the degree to which they have an impact on human rights and commercial law, which might not have been the case in a pre-Internet world.[26]

For businesses providing free public Wi-Fi, there is a potential liability, under section 14 of the DEA, for a £250,000 fine for not policing those systems to Ofcom's satisfaction. This may lead to the withdrawal of such free public Wi-Fi services, if the level of potential liability under section 14 gets widely publicised.

There are questions relating to presumption of guilt—does an ISP customer linked to an IP address tagged as the source of infringement have the burden of proving their innocence; or does the ISP or music company have to prove guilt?

It is possible another member the household, a friend or a neighbour or passerby (taking advantage of an unsecured wireless router) could be the person engaging in the suspected illicit activity.

Does the suspect have access to due process? Do they get to defend themselves in court, in an independent tribunal, or does it all get managed by ISPs and music companies in house? In terms of costs involved, the latter would presumably be the preferred option for industry but not the individual suspect. Is there an appropriate appeal process? How long will an Internet ban last?

With such concerns as burden of proof, due process and access to court, this could be argued to be a criminal justice rather than a civil infringement matter. Indeed the ultimate sanction of disconnection from the Net—curtailment of access to entertainment, commerce, employment, education, freedom of association and speech—seems more like a criminal than a civil penalty. In addition the entire household suffers the burden of disconnection due to the suspected illicit actions of one or a small number of individuals.

So legal questions of proportionality arise—is a three strikes (or 'technical measures') regime a proportionate response to the specific problem? According to the Promusicae vs. Telefonica case in the European Court of Justice (ECJ)[27], the rights of the music labels to protect their copyrights must be balanced with the basic human rights of users of the Internet. It is possible therefore that the ECJ might strike down a three strikes scheme on the grounds of proportionality.

There are also complex questions relating to how a three strikes scheme might come into conflict with EU directives on data protection[28], e-commerce[29] and privacy and electronic communications[30] to name but three. The ISPs have certain protections from liability under the e-commerce directive, for example, as 'mere conduits' of Internet traffic. Whereas the privacy implications of the large scale, potentially indiscriminate monitoring that is required for the implementation of three strikes policies, are significant[31].

The Ignorance of the Policymakers

Many politicians were baffled by the level of public interest in the Digital Economy Bill and the torrent of e-mails they received. Some said it did not matter that they did not understand it as they could always call the experts at the BPI for advice (Lilian Edwards, personal communication). It is a perfectly rational thing to do to ask an expert for advice when you do not understand something and also reasonable to assume the experts in this case reside in the industry. Unfortunately, the issue goes well beyond the specific interests of the recording industry. Consumer or ISP or technology experts, for example, would provide a completely different perspective and multidisciplinary input is a crucially important part of the process if information laws are to be fit for purpose.

Stephen Timms was appointed Minister for Digital Britain in August 2009, at about the same time Peter Mandelson decided there was a pressing need for the government to tackle illicit file sharing. Mr Timms became responsible for the detail of the Digital Economy Bill and for steering it on its passage through the House of Commons. Yet it appears that as late as February 2010, Mr Timms did not understand that the term 'IP address' used in connection with the Internet means Internet Protocol address. In a memo to fellow Labour MP, Emily Thornberry, Mr Timms refers to capturing information about the source of infringing material "including the intellectual property (IP) address along with a date and time stamp"[32]. This was widely seized on by opponents of the Bill as illustrating the government's lack of understanding of the technology they were trying to regulate.

Possibly the best example of the lack of understanding of copyright in the two main parties, Labour and Conservative, that co-operated to rush the Bill through the 'wash-up' process, came during the election campaign. The Labour Party used a poster with a picture of the Conservative leader's head superimposed on the body of a character from a popular BBC drama series *Ashes to Ashes*. The slogan said "Don't let him take Britain back to the 1980s." The Conservatives immediately responded with their own version of the poster and a different slogan, "Fire up the Quattro. It's time for change". Neither party seemed to appreciate the irony of engaging in such copyright infringement whilst going through the process of passing the DEA[33].

CONCLUSIONS

I began this chapter by suggesting that it is not always clear whether policymakers fully understand the complexity or technology of the systems they are attempting to regulate, or the actual effect their regulations will have in practice. The process through which the DEA came into being is a good illustration of that. That type of process, far from being unique, is evident in the stories of the development of numerous information laws and international treaties[34]. There are a number of lessons to draw from the emergence of the DEA, regardless of how it evolves or gets implemented.

First, it seems that, in the UK at least, many policymakers do not under-stand the Internet, how it works and how it is used—that it is more than a game/copying machine/new kind of TV—or how to go about regulating it effectively. That is not a criticism of the policymakers—the electorate choose them in a democracy. Those policymakers must accept their share of culpability but it is more a criticism of the political process, 24/7 sound bite news cycle and the world of short attention spans that spawns such policy-makers. This process makes in-depth, rational public debate, about serious and complex issues, virtually impossible. I would also criticise members of the electorate who do understand the technologies but who do not engage in the political process actively enough and with sufficiently engaging and informative stories to educate policymakers properly about the complex technologies they are attempting to control (Shafak, 2010). Certain special interest stakeholders, on the other hand, have very strong narratives and are highly skilled at engaging policymakers. The result, in the context of information laws, is that some stakeholders have a disproportionate degree of influence.

Second, we need more than well-told stories. Most of the figures that are quoted in relation to industry losses due to copyright infringement on the Internet do not have a sound evidentiary basis. There is a desperate need for sound empirical research, tested to rigorous academic standards, on the effects of the Internet on creativity and commerce in an information age. Not every song copied is a lost sale. It is only a lost sale if the person doing the copying would otherwise have purchased that song. Many teenagers do not have the disposable income to buy all the music they listen to on the Internet, but they often sample and find bands whose range of music they do later buy. Some of the material on the Net is no longer commercially available or is out of copyright or is covered by creative commons licences. The dynamics of all this are nontrivial, and we will not get a better picture of what is really happening until we investigate it properly. Making laws based on sound empirical evidence is likely to be more effective than laws based on stories alone.

Third, transparency in law making is not enough. The making of the DEA was transparent and the engagement of a large number of people in the process through campaigning and social networks was transparent, informative, even shocking to people monitoring our policymakers in real time for the first time. The enforcement of the Act, technical measures and Internet censorship, may or may not be transparent (Marsden, 2010). The DEA has been passed in the hope that a lot of the awkward details can be worked out later e.g. by Ofcom and the Secretary of State.

Finally, information policymaking is too important to be left to ignorant policymakers, specialists and special interests. The Internet and informa-tion laws[35] transcend specialist disciplines and reach into people's lives, in the manner of all complex systems, in unexpected ways.

I doubt that I would have predicted, twenty years ago, that copyright would become a default regulator of access to education, employment, government and commercial services or basic rights related to privacy or freedom of expression. But that is exactly what copyright has become in the Internet age. This previously obscure framework of what would have been industrial regulation—relevant only to those with the capital to invest in printing presses or recording studios or broadcast technology—now applies at the level of the individual with a computer connected to the Internet. It may become a factor in whether we even have access to the Internet.

Who can convince a teenager that some ill-thought-out activity on Facebook might come back to haunt him in ten years when a prospective employer does a background check on the Internet? Information was once scattered, localised, forgettable, contextualised to social norms of those party to it when initially shared. The same information on the Internet is now permanent, detailed, searchable, geographically unbounded, editable, possibly corrosive and prone to being used in ways we would never agree to (such as identity (ID) theft, surveillance or profiling for target marketing or social/political compartmentalisation). Yet the effects of this are too abstract and long term for most of us to register or care about the potential risks.

So we need multidisciplinary stakeholder involvement in the process of making, implementing, monitoring and enforcing information laws. Returning then to the theme of this book, the significance of the DEA story is in the process that is used to make regulations relating to the nature of information. The nature of information in that process and the way that information and associated technologies are conceptualised through narratives (rather than evidence) leads directly to laws. These laws, in turn, govern the nature of information as well as forming the basic rules of the road for our information society. The process is cyclic, flawed, and some even argue that it is broken (Boyle, 2008). So perhaps, in addition to multidisciplinary participation, we may need a digital constitution or bill of rights to set down some basic values and boundaries for those laws and the processes from which they emerge.

I will close with a quote from Paul Krugman (2010):

> When I was young and naïve I believed that important people took positions based on careful consideration of the options. Now I know better.

NOTES

1. I use the phrase 'rules of the road' in a metaphorical sense to cover the default rules of the information society.
2. The report specifically called for "greater balance and flexibility of IP rights to allow individuals, businesses and institutions to use information and ideas in ways consistent with the digital age." At the time of writing, it remains illegal in the UK to copy CDs onto digital music players for personal use.

3. In the summer of 2008, the UK government began a consultation on the EU commission proposal to extend the term of copyright in sound recordings: UK-IPO 18 July 2008 Response to the European Commission's proposal to extend the term of copyright protection. My submission to the consultation is available at Corrigan (2008a). By December 2008 the UK government and Culture Secretary Andy Burnham were enthusiastically supporting the term extension (Ashton, 2008).

4. Haute Autorité pour la diffusion des oeuvres et la protection des droits sur Internet. Also known as the "Création et Internet" law.

5. At the time of writing, no one in France has yet had their Internet services cut off under the HADOPI law. Members of the ruling UMP (Union pour un Mouvement Populaire) party were reportedly concerned that the adoption of HADOPI had damaged their image with the younger generation of French voters. For a good discussion on the state of play with HADOPI, see Jondet (2010).

6. The rules which govern the telecoms sector in the EU were agreed in 2002. These reforms were an attempt to bring those directives up to date e.g. regulating access (2002/19/EC), the regulatory framework (2002/21/EC), authorisation of networks and services (2002/20/EC), universal service and consumer protection requirements (2002/22/EC) and electronic privacy (2002/58/EC).

7. This is slightly over-simplified since a meeting of the culture ministers in November 2008, for example, effectively opposed French proposals on curbing online piracy through compulsory measures against free downloading (Moody, 2008).

8. Monica Horten at IPtegrity.com outlines, in a series of blog posts, the intricate and sometimes crude political games that were involved in the process. The disputed amendment started out as "Amendment 138", then confusingly became "Amendment 46".

9. See Article 1.3(a) of the Telecoms Reform, 'Better Regulation' directive, (Directive 2009/140/EC of the European Parliament and of the Council of 25 November 2009). The Spanish government which was about to assume the presidency of the EU in January 2010 immediately ruled out introducing a three strikes regime in Spain.

10. Independent regulator and competition authority for the UK communications industries.

11. Cox (2009) and Horten (2009) provide further background. I commented on this at the time at Corrigan (2009).

12. A 'Henry VIII clause' in the UK is a term for a clause in an Act that enables primary legislation to be amended by subsequent secondary legislation. It arises from the Statute of Proclamations 1539, used in the time of Henry VIII to legislate by royal proclamation. See Wade and Forsyth (1994), pp.863–864.

13. The conclusions say that writing a law that says three strikes will be implemented without specifying how, why, where, when, by whom, under what authority and what kind of due process and pre-cutoff appeal mechanism will be provided is unacceptable. The committee also criticises the Henry VIII clause.

14. Hansard is the transcript of debates of the UK parliament. Links to various Hansard records of debates on the Act can be found on the website supporting this book, at www.perspectiveson.info.

15. Richard Clayton (2010) argues that such blocking is trivial to circumvent and that the amendment was a bad idea.

16. Davey (2010) discusses the economic rationale of this.

17. See the Register of Lords' Interests at www.publications.parliament.uk/pa/ld/ldreg/reg01.htm. At the time of writing, the Register of Lords Interests

does not specify the level of remuneration Lord Clement-Jones receives from DLA Piper. At the time of the amendment the entry in the register under the sub heading "*12(b) Parliamentary lobbying" said that he was "paid £70,000 in respect of his services as Co-Chairman of DLA Piper's global government relations practice".

18. *Hansard*, 15 Mar 2010, column 458.
19. Liberal Democrat Spring Conference (2010) Emergency Motion: Freedom, Creativity and the Internet.
20. These can be found by visiting www.twitter.com and searching for #debll or #deact.
21. *Hansard*, 7 Apr 2010, col. 1106
22. See http://debillitated.heroku.com/ for a visual summary of the final outcome.
23. *Hansard*, 7 Apr 2010, col. 1115
24. *Hansard*, 6 Apr 2010, col. 867
25. The word 'location' does not seem to be defined anywhere in the Act, though s17(1) refers to "a location on the internet".
26. See, for example, French Conseil constitutionnel (Wednesday 10 June 2009)—Décision N° 2009–580 DC, discussed by Sroussi (2009); see also German Federal Constitutional Court Judgment of 2 March 2010. 1 BvR 256/08, 1 BvR 263/08, 1 BvR 586/08 (discussed by Vermeulen, 2010); also in connection with the censorship provisions of the DEA see the Dutch decision LJN: BN1445 District Court The Hague, 365643 / KG ZA 10–573 (July 2010). In the Dutch case, the Brein Foundation (Protection Rights Entertainment Industry Netherlands) had requested that the court order ISP Ziggo to block the Pirate Bay. The court decided such a ruling would be excessively intrusive and ordered Brein to pay the full costs of the case. At the time of writing Brein have said they will appeal.
27. Productores de Música de España (Promusicae) v. Telefónica de España S.A.U. European Court of Justice (Grand Chamber), Case C-275/06, 2008 CELEX no 62006J0275 (29 January 2008).
28. Directive 95/46/EC of the European Parliament and of the Council of 24 October 1995 on the protection of individuals with regard to the processing of personal data and on the free movement of such data.
29. Directive 2000/31/EC of the European Parliament and of the Council of 8 June 2000 on certain legal aspects of information society services, in particular electronic commerce, in the Internal Market ('Directive on electronic commerce').
30. Directive 2002/58/EC concerning the processing of personal data and the protection of privacy in the electronic communications sector (Directive on privacy and electronic communications) and Directive 2009/136/EC of the European Parliament and of the Council of 25 November 2009 amending Directive 2002/22/EC on universal service and users' rights relating to electronic communications networks and services, Directive 2002/58/EC concerning the processing of personal data and the protection of privacy in the electronic communications sector and Regulation (EC) No 2006/2004 on cooperation between national authorities responsible for the enforcement of consumer protection laws.
31. See, for example, Section IV of the *Opinion of the European Data Protection Supervisor on the current negotiations by the European Union of an Anti-Counterfeiting Trade Agreement (ACTA)* (2010/C 147/03–10).
32. Copies of the memo were leaked and posted on the Internet e.g. at http://i.imgur.com/1pXlO.jpg
33. The Labour Party released their version of the poster on 2 April 2010, five days before the DEA was passed. See Hennessy (2010).

34. Including the TRIPS, numerous EU directives, 1996 WIPO treaties, Digital Millennium Copyright Act. See Drahos with Braithwaite (2002).
35. I have not mentioned the impact of intellectual property on access to medicines but for a stark illustration of the life-changing impact of a special interest dominated, international intellectual property landscape, see 'T Hoen (2010).

BIBLIOGRAPHY

Arthur, C. (2010) 'Controversial Digital Economy Bill Amendment Follows Lobbyists' Draft', *The Guardian* online, http://www.guardian.co.uk/technology/2010/mar/11/digital-economy-bill-amendment-lobbyists (Accessed 28 July 2010).
Ashton, R. (2008) 'Government Signals Extension to Copyright Term', *Music Week*. http://www.musicweek.com/story.asp?storyCode=1036431 (accessed 20 January 2011).
Barnett, E. (2010) 'Pressure Mounts on Digital Economy Bill', *Daily Telegraph* online, http://www.telegraph.co.uk/technology/news/7558967/Pressure-mounts-on-Digital-Economy-Bill.html (Accessed 28 July 2010).
BBC News (2009), *Net Pirates to Be 'Disconnected'*, http://news.bbc.co.uk/1/hi/8328820.stm (Accessed 28 July 2010).
BIS (2009) Consultation Document on Legislation to Address Illicit P2P Filesharing, London, Department of Business, Innovation and Skills.
Boyle, J (1996) *Shamans, Software and Spleens: Law and the Construction of the Information Society*. Cambridge, Massachusetts, Harvard University Press.
Boyle, J. (2008) *The Public Domain: Enclosing the Commons of the Mind*, Yale University Press, New Haven and London.
Carter, S. (2009) *Digital Britain: Final Report*, London, Department for Culture, Media and Sport and Department for Business, Innovation and Skills.
Cellan-Jones, R. (2010) 'Digital Economy: The Mandelson letters', *BBC News online*, http://www.bbc.co.uk/blogs/thereporters/rorycellanjones/2010/03/digital_economy_the_mandelson.html (Accessed 28 July 2010).
Clayton, R. (2010) 'A Wrecking Amendment?', *Light Blue Touchpaper blog*, http://www.lightbluetouchpaper.org/2010/03/11/a-wrecking-amendment/ (Accessed 28 July 2010).
Corrigan, R. and Rogers, M. (2005) 'The Economics of Copyright', *World Economics*, Vol. 6, no. 3, pp.153–174.
Corrigan, R. (2008a) 'Comments on Proposed EU Extension of Copyright Term in Sound Recordings', *B2fxxx blog*, http://b2fxxx.blogspot.com/2008/08/uk-ipo-consultation-on-eu-copyright.html (Accessed 28 July 2010).
Corrigan, R. (2008b) *UK Copyright: How It Compares Internationally and Who Are the Winners and Losers*, Westminster eForum, Intellectual Property and the Future of Copyright.
Corrigan, R. (2009), Untitled, *B2fxxx blog*, http://b2fxxx.blogspot.com/2009/07/digital-britain-3-strikes-plans-to.html (Accessed 28 July 2010).
Cox, H. (2009) 'The Devil's in the Digital', *1709 blog*, http://the1709blog.blogspot.com/2009/07/devils-in-digital.html (Accessed 28 July 2010).
Davey, F. (2010) 'New Amendment Gives Copyright Owners a Blank Cheque for Web Censorship', Blog Posting, http://www.francisdavey.co.uk/2010/03/new-amendment-gives-copyright-owners.html (Accessed 28 July 2010).
Drahos, P. with Braithwaite, J. (2002) *Information Feudalism: Who Owns the Knowledge Society*. London, Earthscan.
Edwards, L. (2010a) 'Third Reading DEB', *panGloss* blog, http://blogscript.blogspot.com/2010/03/third-reading-deb.html (Accessed 28 July 2010).

Edwards, L. (2010b) 'Law and Sausages: How Not to Legislate for the Digital Economy', talk at Sheffield Cafe Scientitfique, 20 March 2010.

GAO (2010) Intellectual Property: Observations on Efforts to Quantify the Economic Effects of Counterfeit and Pirated Goods (GAO-10–423), Washington DC, US Government Accountability Office.

Goldacre, B. (2009) 'Illegal Downloads and Dodgy Figures', *The Guardian (London)*, 6 June, p.16.

Gowers, A. (2006) *Gowers Review of Intellectual Property*, London, Her Majesty's Stationery Office.

Gowers, A. (2008) 'Copyright Extension Is Out of Tune with Reality', *Financial Times*, http://www.ft.com/cms/s/0/ba280756-ca07–11dd-93e5–000077b07658. html (Accessed 28 July 2010).

Gyford, P. (2010) 'This Is an Outrage', *Phil Gyford's website*, http://www.gyford. com/phil/writing/2010/04/08/debill.php (Accessed 28 July 2010).

Hennessy, P. (2010) 'Yes, Call Me Gene, Says Cameron', *Daily Telegraph (London)*, 4 April, p.7.

Horten, M. (2009) 'What Are 'Legitimate Reasons' for the UK to Block the Net?', *IPtegrity blog*,http://www.iptegrity.com/index.php?option=com_content&task =view&id=371&Itemid=9 (Accessed 28 July 2010).

Johnson, B. (2010) 'Lords Angered over Three Strikes Rule for Filesharers', *The Guardian (online)*, http://www.guardian.co.uk/technology/2010/mar/02/digital-economy-puttnam (Accessed 28 July 2010).

Joint Committee on Human Rights (2010), *Legislative Scrutiny: Digital Economy Bill (HL Paper 44 / HC 327)*, London, The Stationery Office.

Jondet, N. 'The French Copyright Authority (HADOPI), the Graduated Response and the Disconnection of Illegal File-Sharers' *Gikii V conference*, Edinburgh University, June 2010.

Knights, M. (2007) 'France Takes on P2P Downloaders', *ITPro*, http://www.itpro. co.uk/141720/france-takes-on-p2p-downloaders (Accessed 28 July 2010).

Krugman, P. (2010) 'Myths of Austerity', *New York Times*, 2 July, p.25.

Lessig, L. (1999) *Code and Other Laws of Cyberspace*, New York, Basic Books.

Lessig, L (2001) The Future of Ideas: The Fate of the Commons in a Connected World. New York, Random House.

Lipstadt, D. (1994) Denying the Holocaust: The Growing Assault on Truth and Memory. London, Penguin.

Litman, J. (2001) *Digital Copyright*. New York, Prometheus Books.

Mandelson, P. (2009) 'Taking Something for Nothing Is Wrong. . . . ', *The Times (London)*, 29 August, p.20.

Marsden, C.T. (2010) *Net Neutrality: Towards a Co-Regulatory Solution*. London, Bloomsbury Academic.

Moody, G. (2008) '"Three Strikes and You're Out" Struck Down', *Open . . . blog*, http://opendotdotdot.blogspot.com/2008/11/three-strikes-and-youre-out-struck-down.html (Accessed 28 July 2010).

Oliver, J. (2009) 'Mandelson Targets Web Pirates after Dinner with Mogul', *Sunday Times (London)*, 16 August, p.9.

Shafak, E. (2010) 'The Politics of Fiction', *TED Global Conference*, Oxford, July 2010.

Sroussi, G. (2009), 'France—The Hadopi Law and France's Controversial Fight Against Piracy', *Linklaters Technology, Media and Telecommunications News*, http://www.linklaters.com/Publications/Publication1403Newsletter/20091016/ Pages/FranceTheHadopiLaw.aspx (Accessed 28 July 2010).

'T Hoen, E. (2010) 'A Proposal for Change: Managing Patents to ensure Access to AIDS Medicines for All'. AIDS 2010 IAS Conference, Vienna, 21 July 2010.

Topping, A. (2009) 'One Step Forward, Two Steps back as Rock Star Alliance Wades into Filesharing Debate', *The Guardian*, 3 September, p.13.

Van Kranenburg, R. (2008) The Internet of Things: A Critique of Ambient Technology and the All-Seeing Network of RFID, Amsterdam, Institute of Network Cultures.

Vermeulen, M. (2010) 'Germany Federal Constitutional Court Overturns Data Retention Law', *The Lift* blog, http://legalift.wordpress.com/2010/03/04/germany-federal-constitutional-court-overturns-data-retention-law/ (Accessed 28 July 2010).

Wade, H.W.R. and Forsyth, C.F. (1994) *Administrative Law* (7th ed.), Oxford, Clarendon Press.

Wintour, P. (2010) 'Interview: 'Sometimes True Loyalty Comes from Disagreeing'', *The Guardian (London)*, 16 July, p.14.

Wray, R. (2010) 'Online Piracy Law Unlikely to face Major Scrutiny', *The Guardian (London)*, 16 March, p.23.

12 Conclusion

David Chapman and Magnus Ramage

Hans Christian von Baeyer described 'information' as the new language of science (von Baeyer, 2003). That idea is witnessed by Chapter 10 of this book, where Nixon has discussed some ways in which quantum mechanics brushes up against information concepts. The language of information is used increasingly in fields outside science, however, and other chapters of this book have explored a number of them.

There is today a research effort directed at deriving a unified theory of information (see, for example, Hofkirchner, 2010), but this book has no such ambition. Our aims in this book are somewhat more modest: our goal is to share insights between disciplines in the hope of learning from one another so that we can speak the language of information more fluently.

Information is in a curious position academically—many different disciplines feel that they 'own' the concept, yet there is little common dialogue between the disciplines. It is our contention that any common view of information can only arise through the study of the multiple perspectives on information found in these many disciplines that hold it to be central. Rather than seeking a grand theory, therefore, this final brief chapter draws attention to a few 'family resemblances' between the disciplinary perspectives described in the different chapters that might provide some helpful insights into what it is people mean when they use the language of information.

Four broad themes that arise in several of the chapters are context; meaning (and thus the centrality of human beings), dialogue (in many cases as part of a game) and the dynamic nature of information. It is worth noting that the different chapters do not treat these themes in the same way and in some cases do not agree with each other—there are ongoing debates in a number of areas.

CONTEXT

Perhaps the most universal theme is the importance of context. Ramage in Chapter 2 emphasises the role of context as one of the distinctive features of the soft view of information, distinguishing it from the hard view. According to Chapman in Chapter 4, however, context is fundamental to the hard view too, albeit a 'hard' context of, for example, an American Standard Code for Information Interchange (ASCII). The contrasting soft context includes meaning, people and mental processes. Chapman makes a link between hard information and semiotic signs, which is also the starting point of Monk in Chapter 5. Monk points out that Saussure's signs are arbitrary, held in place by accustomed use—another aspect of context.

In Chapter 3, Bissell quotes a definition of information from an Open University course, which is 'data in context'. Context in Bissell's chapter, however, is important on a different level as well, since his historical perspective draws attention to the way in which the concept of information has developed over time. The need to take account of time is explicit in the definition of information quoted in Chapter 6 by Holwell: data plus meaning (interpretation) in a particular context at a particular time. Within that definition, position in time is distinguished from context, but from another perspective time is merely another dimension of context.

Likewise, the concept of exformation in Chapter 7 by Lefrere arises from the fact that communication takes place within a context. The context holds the exformation, and communication is not understood by an onlooker who lacks the exformation.

Ramage talked about Hayles' image of information being "simultaneously disembodied and reified", and Foster-Jones' exploration of the changing role of libraries and librarians in Chapter 8 is in effect a case study of that process. The physical books and libraries that housed them provided information with a 'body' which it no longer needs, but libraries and librarians still deal in information: it is just the context that has changed.

Piwek in Chapter 9 presents three principles of information flow, the first two of which are explicitly about context: "Information flow = context change"; and "Information flow is context-dependent". For Piwek, information is inextricably bound up with context.

The issues of information policy making addressed by Corrigan in Chapter 11 have come about because of the changing context of information, the disembodiment and the consequent freeing of information explored by Foster-Jones.

One of the most counter-intuitive insights of quantum mechanics is the way in which the observer influences the outcome of observation, as explained by Nixon. This makes a qualitative change in how we can understand the concept of 'context', since the context can now never, even in principle, be a passive backdrop. The information and the context are parts of the same system.

MEANING

We have noted that people are often part of the context, but it is worth noting explicitly that information in all of the chapters, somewhere along the line, involves people and has something to do with meaning.

Monk says that "information needs people" and that information in contexts other than that of human intercourse is used in an anthropomorphic sense. Similarly, Holwell says in the context of her "data, capta, information, knowledge" schema: "the act of creating information is a human act". Shannon information, hard information in the language of Ramage, at first sight has no need of people, and Bissell points out that this distance from people, and therefore from meaning, was a reason for some people to object to Shannon's use of the word 'information'. Chapman however argues that we can use the language of meaning even for hard information. Perhaps this is an anthropomorphic use of the word, but in that case what we have done is brought people back in to the picture.

Ramage's soft information is explicitly about people. For Bissell, aspects of the very concept of information are socially constructed; Lefrere embeds information in communities; and the contexts of Piwek are the people who populate the dialogues he presents.

Foster-Jones writes of the people of libraries—the librarians and customers—but could the information of the books have an independent existence? Could we envisage a library with books that are never read? Perhaps that thought experiment is sufficient to discard the idea of a library without people. Certainly Chapter 8 is about people and information. A similar comment might be made about Corrigan's look at information policy making. The issues are very much human issues, but does that mean that information involves people? Maybe, in fact, the changes of technology have unleashed the issues addressed by Corrigan precisely because information involves people.

Perhaps, though, it is in Nixon's chapter about quantum theory that the idea of information ever *not* involving people is finally banished for good. The inextricable involvement of the observer in the physical (quantum-mechanical) world simply doesn't allow for information—for anything—that doesn't involve people.

DIALOGUE AND GAMES

It has been taken for granted from the start that information is about communication, and there is no need to explore that further. Of more interest, however, is the extent to which information is associated with dialogue of some sort and/or with games.

Piwek's chapter was explicitly about dialogue and games, but they are also mentioned in passing or are implicit in a number of other chapters. Monk talks about Wittgenstein's language games and Lefrere of von Neumann's use of the metaphor of a game. In all cases, meaning is communicated through the use of dialogue, and the aspect of a game comes about because of the semi-formal rules surrounding the dialogue.

Of particular interest to Foster-Jones is the impact and opportunities of 'Web 2.0' on libraries. Web 2.0 is about the creation of a 'return channel' on the Web, so that the user of the Web can have participate in a dialogue rather than be the recipient of broadcast information. In this sense, a library used to one-way, broadcasting, information now has the possibility of entering into a dialogue with the user.

Dialogue and games—often of a particularly confrontational nature—also characterise the development of information policy as recounted by Corrigan.

It is interesting to note that 'mechanical' dialogue is a requirement of all but the most trivial of digital communication systems. The set-up of a communication channel invariably involves what is referred to as a 'handshake' when the two ends of the channel establish the basic parameters of the communication. The procedures needed to establish secure communication using quantum cryptography as described by Nixon involve a handshake of this nature.

INFORMATION AS A DYNAMIC CONCEPT

Several chapters discuss the dynamics of information—the way in which its nature changes over time. The dimension of time is explicit in Holwell's definition of information ("*data* plus *meaning* (interpretation) in a particular *context* at a particular *time*"). The dimension of time is inherent in dialogues and games, indeed, in any communication.

Foster-Jones, with her broad historical overview of the changing role of libraries as store-houses and gatekeepers of information, shows that, within this area, the way information is understood has changed significantly over time and in particular has become more clearly seen as an entity in its own right rather than a property of a physical object such as a book. Corrigan presents an overview of a much shorter time period but likewise looks at the way understandings of information have developed significantly, through the interaction between the creators and users of the Internet, government bodies and copyright owners.

Ramage and Bissell both present intellectual histories of the development of information within particular academic fields—cybernetics and communications—and both discuss the way the concept of information has changed over time. Interestingly, Bissell argues that the *rhetoric* around changing information technologies has remained remarkably constant—the techno-utopian view, that the world is changing rapidly and miraculously. Nixon also presents a historical overview of a changing intellectual history that is inexorably bound up with information—the perplexing and paradoxical developments in quantum theory.

Each of these chapters, in their different ways, show that information is frequently not a static concept, but rather something that changes and develops over time within the particular social and historical context of an academic field.

OTHER THEMES

Some further notable themes that are important to more than one chapter, although not universally, are the concept of difference and making a difference, the idea of information being for a purpose and the primacy of language in information.

Ramage quoted Bateson's famous definition of information as "the difference that makes a difference". While difference has not been discussed explicitly in other chapters, difference is key to a number of topics, and is intimately associated with context. We might, for example, talk in terms of difference for the sets of messages described by Chapman or for the eigenstates of Nixon.

The other part of Bateson's definition, making a difference, has arguably figured even more prominently in several chapters and links with the idea that information is associated with purpose. This theme was most explicit in Holwell's discussion of information systems, which she described as existing to support purposeful action. There is also a parallel between Holwell's distinction between data and capta and Lefrere's concept of exformation. Both sets of concepts are to do with identifying the part of data that is useful—the part that can make a difference or has a purpose. We can also equate 'making a difference' to context change; we can see this theme in Piwek's chapter too. Corrigan, with his focus on the role of information to change society, likewise, clearly can be seen in terms of making a difference—as he eloquently writes about copyright (which is nothing more than a regulatory mechanism of the transmission of information), it has "become a default regulator of access to education, employment, government and commercial services".

Piwek's chapter is about language, and most of the chapters implicitly assume that they are concerned first and foremost with language. The possible exception is Nixon with his focus on quantum information. Certain other chapters have their focus on language but could be considered to have extension to other areas. In particular, the information systems of Holwell could be concerned with numerical information, and while the layer model of Chapman is described in terms of conveying words, it works equally well for numbers, images or sounds. Nonetheless, for most of the chapters, information is taken as something that is expressed through language, which, in turn, represents and supports language. In many ways, language is as much an information technology as the computer has ever been.

It is perhaps worth observing that many of themes discussed in this book are ones that might be found in texts from the field of semiotics. In this book Chapman and especially Monk have made links between information and semiotics. It is certainly not a new insight, but maybe it is a reminder of one of the intellectual resources that might have increasing importance if we find the language of information permeating an ever-widening range of disciplines.

We began this book by observing that "everything is information, and information is everything". Through the chapters in the book, we hope we have shown that information is also *everywhere*—in very many different academic disciplines and pervasive throughout society—but also that information is a contested and complex concept, which simple and single-discipline models are insufficient to understand. We need diversity of perspectives and ways of thought if we are to make sense of this ultra-familiar yet curiously elusive concept of information.

BIBLIOGRAPHY

Hofkirchner, W. (2010) *Twenty Questions about a Unified Theory of Information*, Litchfield Park, Arizona, Emergent Publications.

von Baeyer, H.C. (2003) *Information: The New Language of Science*, London, Weidenfeld and Nicolson.

Contributors

Chris Bissell is Professor of Telematics, a Fellow of the Institution of Engineering and Technology and a Fellow of the Higher Education Academy. He has been responsible for Open University (OU) teaching materials on telecommunications, control engineering, media studies, and other ICT topics. He was Head of the Information and Communication Technologies (ICT) Department for nine years from 1996 onwards. His major research interests are in the history of technology, mathematical modelling and engineering education, on which he has published widely. He is also active in quality assurance in higher education.

David Chapman is a Senior Lecturer in Information and Communication Technologies at the Open University, a Fellow of the Institution of Engineering and Technology and a Fellow of the Higher Education Academy. Before joining the OU he worked on optical fibre communication systems with Plessey Telecommunications, and his PhD investigated optical fibre networks. His current main research interest is in the nature of information, and he maintains a blog on the subject at http://intropy. co.uk/.

Ray Corrigan is a Senior Lecturer in Technology at the OU and author of *Digital Decision Making: Back to the Future* (Springer, 2007). He wrote the OU's Internet law course, as well as a variety of other materials on the environment and information and communications technologies. Ray blogs random thoughts on law, the Internet and society at http:// b2fxxx.blogspot.com/. Before alighting in academia, he spent nearly ten years in a variety of roles in industry.

Juanita Foster-Jones, MAODE (Open) BA FHEA MCLIP, is a chartered librarian and worked at the OU Library from 2000–2008. At the OU she worked with the Information Literacy Unit, as an author and online moderator for TU120 *Beyond Google* course. She also researched the use of web conferencing to deliver information literacy skills training and development. Prior to that Juanita was a project officer on the DiVA

(Digital Video Applications) project, where she designed the metadata scheme and contributed to the design of the DiVA interface and help systems. She has co-authored papers on metadata and the DiVA system. Juanita currently works as a Teaching Fellow at the Department of Information Studies, Aberystwyth University.

Sue Holwell was a Senior Lecturer in Information Systems at the OU until her retirement. She is interested in the conceptual clarity of information systems thinking and the use of systems thinking in Information Systems (IS).

Paul Lefrere is a Senior Research Fellow at the OU and visiting Professor of e-learning at the University of Tampere in Finland. As well as developing OU course materials on a wide range of subjects, he has led numerous multi-partner research projects on technology-enhanced learning and related topics and published widely on knowledge management and strategic issues. He is the co-author of a globally popular book on transforming e-knowledge and of influential papers on horizon scanning and on action analytics. He advises ministries, the European Commission and leading multinational companies.

John Monk is a Chartered Engineer and Emeritus Professor at the OU with an interest in the philosophy of technology and the professionalism of engineers.

Tony Nixon is a Senior Lecturer in Information Systems at the OU; he is a former Head of the Systems Department, which he joined in 2002, and his current research is in the field of X-ray Photoelectron Spectroscopy. He also has an interest in open source teaching and was a founder member of the University's Open Source Teaching Group in 1999.

Paul Piwek is a Lecturer in the Department of Computing at the OU whose research interest is formal theories of information with applications in dialogue modelling and automatic natural language generation.

Magnus Ramage is a Lecturer in Information Systems in the Communication and Systems Department at the OU. His research has three main strands: the nature of information, the history of the field of systems thinking (and related areas such as cybernetics) and the evolution of information systems over time. He is co-author of *Systems Thinkers* (Springer, 2009) with Karen Shipp and co-editor of *Online Communication and Collaboration: A Reader* (Routledge, 2010) with Helen Donelan and Karen Kear.

Index